THE PLEASURE IS ALL MINE

THE

Pleasure

— IS —

ALL MINE

SELFISH FOOD FOR
MODERN LIFE

SUZANNE PIRRET

WILLIAM MORROW

An Imprint of **HarperCollins***Publishers*

HarperCollins books may be purchased for educational, business, or sales promotional use. For information please write: Special Markets Department, HarperCollins Publishers, 10 East 53rd Street, New York, NY 10022.

FIRST EDITION

Designed by Gretchen Achilles

Library of Congress Cataloging-in-Publication Data

Pirret, Suzanne.
    The pleasure is all mine : selfish food for modern life / Suzanne Pirret. — 1st ed.
      p.   cm.
    Includes index.
    ISBN 978-0-06-168712-9
    1. Cookery for one.   2. Cookery, International.   I. Title.
TX652.P575   2009
641.5'61–dc22   2008038538

09 10 11 12 13 WBC/RRD 10 9 8 7 6 5 4 3 2 1

To the memory of my dad, Joe

and

For my mom, Millie

CONTENTS

Introduction   xv

THE SICK HANDSHAKE
GETTING A RESERVATION IN ANY LANGUAGE
1

Best Steak au Poivre with Frites 8

Best Mac 'n' Cheese 11

Best Braised Lamb Shank 12

Best Chicken Pot Pie 14

Best Duck Confit 17

Best Crab Cakes 20

Best Pork Chops and Applesauce 22

Best Fish & Chips 24

THE CRUEL REVENGE OF GENERAL TSAO
HOW TO MAKE TAKE-OUT
27

CHINESE   30

General Tsao's Chicken 30

Cold Sesame Noodles 32

Crispy Duck with Warm Fresh Plum Sauce 33

INDIAN   35

Coconut Fish Curry...35

Home-Style Yellow Split Peas 36

Homemade Naan Bread...37

THAI   39

Jasmin's Pad Thai..39

Tom Yum Kung Soup..42

Grilled Lamb Chops with Lemongrass...................................43

FAST FOOD   45

Pizza Margherita (not Domino's)..45

Fried Chicken with Buttermilk Biscuits (not KFC's) 48

Quarter Pounder with Fries (not McDonald's)....................51

DINNER GUESTS

WHEN TO DELETE THEM FROM YOUR PHONE

53

Three-Cheese Ravioli with Shaved White Truffles 60

Roasted Lobster...62

Pan-Seared Wagyu Steak..65

Sea Urchin Risotto 66

Croque Monsieur with Smoked Salmon and Caviar..........68

Escalope of Foie Gras with Wild

Mushrooms and Aged Balsamic 70

"YOU WANNA KNOW HOW I GOT THESE SCARS?"
HOW TO LOOK (AND COOK) LIKE A BADASS
73

Calamar Relleno con Setas y Vegetales.............................78

Clips de Cogollos con Mango 80

Ristretto di Piselli con Gnocchetti di Pane all'Uva e

Fresco di Capra 84

Soft-Shell Crabs with Lima Bean Salad, Grilled Bacon,

and Cornbread...87

Grilled Peaches with Amaretto 90

ON GRAZING
91

Wild Sea Bream Seviche 97

Sea Scallops with Seaweed Butter............................98

Bacalao Croquettes with Aioli................................100

Carpaccio of Beef, Pecorino, and Black Olives.................102

Wild Mushrooms on Grilled Ciabatta with Garlic

Lemon Aioli...103

Pissaladière 104

Zucchini Fritters with Dill......................................106

Yellowtail Sashimi with Green Apple and

Yuzu Dipping Sauce...107

Grilled Sardine Panzanella......................................108

Vietnamese Summer Rolls.......................................110

Frisée with Manchego Cheese, Roasted Marcona

Almonds, and Quince Dressing 112

Basquian Lemon Shrimp 113

SUZIE MANNERS'S GUIDE TO MODERN ETIQUETTE

115

BREAD   120

Homemade Parker House Rolls 120

SOUP   122

Classic Winter Vegetable Soup 122

SPAGHETTI (OR ANY LONG PASTA)   124

Pasta alla Bottarga 124

Tagliatelle with Black Truffles 126

LITTLE BONY BIRDS   128

Grilled Spatchcocked Spiced Quail 128

SHELLFISH   130

Cazuela de Arroz Langoustines 130

EAT YOUR GREENS!   132

Three Ways 132

JUST MESSY   134

A Big Ol' Burger 134

BRUNCH: WHY?

137

Blueberry Pancakes 141

Scrambled Eggs 142

Home-Cured Gravlax with Bagels and Cream Cheese ... 144

Fried Duck Egg with Guanciale and Toast........................146

Frittata con delle Erbe..147

Warm Beignets..148

BLT on Toasted Brioche with Garlic Aioli........................150

Sixties Granola..151

WASTE MANAGEMENT

BECAUSE THERE'S NO SUCH THING AS LEFTOVER DESSERT

153

One Big Profiterole..158

Crêpes Suzette 160

Fresh Pineapple Tarte Tatin 162

Cake 164

Lemon-Lime Gelato 165

Warm Banana Toffee Mille-Feuille................................166

Apple Turnover 168

"There-is-no-way-in-hell-I-am-waiting-in-line-for-two-
hours" Cupcakes 170

Pignoli Biscotti..171

Butterscotch Panna Cotta with Roasted Macadamia
Nut Praline 172

Wild Blueberry Tart..174

Affogato..176

AN HOMAGE TO WILLY WONKA

177

Warm Chocolate Fondant..181

Peanut Butter Cups 183

A Brownie..184

Melt-in-Your-Mouth Chocolate Cookies 186

Valrhona Chocolate Truffles.. 187

Chocolate Ice Cream Float 191

Bread and Chocolate 192

MÉNAGE À DEUX

193

BONUS RECIPES

197

DUCK CONFIT   197

Duck Ragu with Papparadelle... 197

Duck Rillette 197

Foie Gras Stuffing... 198

BACALAO (SALT COD)   199

Baked Salt Cod Fillet 199

Bacalao with Fresh Orange and Black Olives..................... 199

BAKED POTATOES   200

Gnocchi.. 200

DUCK FAT   200

LEMONGRASS   201

Mussels in Lemongrass Broth... 201

Steamed Fish 201

GUANCIALE   202

Pasta con Guanciale e Prezzemolo.......................................202

SCRAPS OF PASTA DOUGH   203

Scialatielli con Pomodori Ciliege Arrosti 203

SEVEN USES FOR EXTRA MASCARPONE OR
CRÈME FRAÎCHE   203

HERBS   204

Pistou/Pesto...204
Salsa Verde 204
Salad 205
A Mojito...205
The Toby Cecchini 206

YOUR BARE-BONES CUPBOARD

207

ON DRINKING ALONE

AN INTERVIEW WITH COLUM SHEEHAN

211

Sources   217
Acknowledgments   221
Index   223

INTRODUCTION

ALONE, adj. In bad company.

—AMBROSE BIERCE, *The Devil's Dictionary,* 1911

I'm not sure why eating alone has gotten such a bad rap. With the number of singles, loners, and suicide bombers out there, you'd think it would be fairly acceptable. The images in most cookbooks and cooking shows nowadays help perpetuate the feeling that eating alone—especially eating *well* alone—is not really an option. The requisite denouement for almost all cooking shows includes a fantastically happy group of friends and family, heads thrown back in laughter with the mandatory Mmmmmms, Oohs, and Ahhhhhs, as they feast on the perfect spread—all in blissful, panoramic Technicolor. Your only hope is to be a part of that life one day—or at least experience it with some regularity. But until then, it's antidepressants and beans on toast for your sorry ass.

But to be perfectly honest, some of my best meals have been eaten on my own and some of my worst with other people. Recently, a colleague begged me to join her for dinner at one of my favorite restaurants in London. As we sat at the bar facing into the magical kitchen, the small plates of perfection began to arrive in front of us.

Immediately, she began to dump portions of her food onto my plate and then scrape mine onto hers. All of the exquisitely crafted flavors and meticulously detailed presentations morphed into...Iberico ham thrown over langoustines with foie gras smeared in; chorizo oil dripping over frogs' legs and into osetra caviar; and all infused with a potpourri of summer truffles, quatre épices, jasmine, garlic, seaweed, and something spicy.

I love sharing, but this was desecration.

She then gesticulated loudly and in graphic detail about the outrageous sex acts of her torrid affair as she continued to destroy each plate. The man seated half an inch to her right pretended not to notice. In fact, everyone around us pretended not to notice. No one was really that interested, and all were embarrassed by her selfishness.

As she slobbered on, food spilling out of her mouth, licking her fingers, hair dangling over and into her plate, I can honestly say I did not enjoy my meal. The simple and great pleasure of sharing had been ruined. I kick myself for not just taking her to McDonald's.

How do you say to your dining companion that they're making you sick? I swallowed my American Express bill and vowed never to dine with her again, but only after casually pouring a glass of water down her leg and gracefully knocking back the stool. With her on it.

As a New Yorker relocated to London, I quickly learned that dining out alone just hasn't taken off. I tried it—at a litany of posh and not-so-posh restaurants—but I think I was usually mistaken for a hooker. A hungry hooker.

Forced to retreat back to my flat, I was faced with some stark choices. I began experimenting with take-out (or "take-away"), but I could never properly digest the cardboard pizza with fake cheese and ketchup sauce. The Brazilian delivery boy looked far tastier.

I'd always enthusiastically accept every dinner party invitation extended to me. Some superb, some putrid. As they'd be serving potted shrimp mixed with decade-old dried dill, I'd begin plotting my after-dinner dinner. But based on the contents of my refrigerator, it would be air and gin.

I even offered to prepare a meal for a love interest now and then, but always with the intent that he'd turn down my offer. I mean, you tell me—stay home and cook, or Gordon Ramsay's tasting menu at Royal Hospital Road . . . new season spring lamb at The River Cafe . . . dim sum and cucumber cocktails at Hakkasan . . . or a simple yet perfectly executed milk-fed veal chop at Le Caprice? I was having a ton of fun until a piranha-like spinster snapped, "Stop whoring yourself for dinner." Ouch. Who said sex was involved?

Perhaps it was time for a change.

Nothing sounds more depressing than cooking for one. Where's the excitement in that? The cookbooks out there only exacerbate the mood: a cover photo of an airbrushed chicken breast smothered in an eighties-style cream sauce with three measly turned vegetables makes me want to slit my wrists. What's up with *Vegan for One*? Should it really be titled: *No Meat, No Eggs. No Friends*? What about the cover showing an overdressed dining table with a place setting for (weep weep) one? Menu suggestions, anyone? How about leftovers that can be recycled for days and days—as if you have no life and collect food stamps for a living? Example (based on one whole chicken):

MONDAY: Chicken Véronique (one breast)

TUESDAY: Chicken Oriental (second breast)

WEDNESDAY: Chicken Salad Sandwiches (legs)

THURSDAY: Chicken Wings with Blue Cheese Dressing

FRIDAY: Chicken Soup (from bones and scraps)

SATURDAY: Chicken Livers, marinated in a jar

Note: Reserve all innards and gizzards. If not for yourself, then for your pets.

By Sunday, I'd curl myself up into a pan, douse myself with olive oil, shove some rosemary in my mouth, and throw myself in the oven.

The christening of my kitchen went off in style. I decided it would be more about the spirit. Think Holly Golightly meets Cabiria. Oh crap, Cabiria was a hooker. But a cute one, nonetheless, and styled by her husband, Fellini. I dusted off the bottle of 1970 Mouton Rothschild (with the sweet Chagall drawing at the top of the label) that I had been saving for that perfect occasion to celebrate (which has never happened). Not only was that little relic past its prime drinking years, but my decanter . . . well, actually, I don't have a decanter. So I poured myself a glass, spat out a few pieces of sediment, and began to cook.

I usually cook while on the phone and eat while standing over the sink. But this time I wanted to set the stage. First: the music. It needed to be loud. My downstairs neighbor was a big eighties rock star, so if I blasted his music, no one would complain. Lighting was also key. Bright, so that I didn't chop off my fingers, but flattering. I hate feeling like a hag when I'm cooking. And then, a half a bottle of wine later, I got my *mise* together.

My first meal was steak. No questions asked. As my wine continued to gasp for air, my hefty filet of a beautifully marbled twenty-one-day dry-aged longhorn steak lay out naked—alongside the bottle of wine, to take the chill out of it. I decided that it would be as fancy as that scene with Mia Farrow cooking in *Rosemary's Baby*. Steak into hot pan, two seconds, flip, two seconds more, onto plate, eat.

So, I rubbed my steak with a little oil and sprinkled lots of crushed Maldon salt and cracked black pepper onto both sides. More oil into a frying pan heated at the highest flame until the smoke alarm went off, whereby I promptly removed the battery. Steak into the pan, where it sizzled like a lunatic. I thought at this point I should toss together a crisp green salad to make the look complete, but I didn't feel like it. Sautéed mushrooms? A reduction with veal stock? A simple béarnaise? Perhaps a little Dijon mustard? It just seemed so perfect unadorned. I didn't have those ingredients anyway. I flipped my steak. The crust was deeply caramelized and glistening. I added a little butter for mere decadence and spooned it over the top. After several more minutes, I took it out to rest.

I plopped down on my floor and ate it with one hand. I'm really a cavewoman at heart.

So that was how it began. Now I treasure my solitude. My privacy. To prepare an exquisite meal for myself—even if it's a plate of cheeses and charcuterie—is peaceful bliss. Of course, it'd be with a hunk of fresh Poilâne, a handful of cornichons, a few spoonfuls of an interesting chutney, and a nice little tumbler of chilled Brouilly, but it's beautiful. Because in the end, it's only a meal.

This is a cookbook about cooking for yourself, decadently. There are serious cookbooks written by serious chefs and light and breezy cookbooks written by wholesome cooks. This is both. It's naughty and doesn't take itself too seriously.

And because I hate cleaning up, there is *no* fancy equipment involved—no KitchenAid, food processor, blender, pasta machine, ice cream maker, Pacojet, VacUpack, iSi gourmet whipper, blowtorch, safety goggles, pressure cooker, deep-fat fryer, thermometer, Japanese mandoline, larding needle, or sous chef necessary. Minimal mess/exquisite meal.

Each chapter begins with a short story based on my experiences living in New York, Los Angeles, Paris, and London followed by my repertoire of recipes that have been inspired by modern classics, some great chefs, my travels, and, I might add, a fair amount of successful experimentation. They're all for one serving and written in a fairly simple style. Most are paired with a superb wine selection suggested by the astoundingly gifted sommelier Colum Sheehan of Babbo Ristorante and Enoteca in New York City. Think solitude at its most celebratory.

THE PLEASURE IS ALL MINE

THE SICK HANDSHAKE

GETTING A RESERVATION IN ANY LANGUAGE

To some extent, restaurants did replace nightclubs, and restaurant-going became a kind of competitive sport...being able to get reservations in a particular place is an indicator of your position in the [Manhattan] social hierarchy.

—JAY MCINERNEY in *The Observer* (London)

NEW YORK CITY

It's 8:30 P.M. and while I'm walking into a restaurant in the meat-packing district (not my first choice), two women knock me over as they make their way to the host stand.

"But, like we just wanna couple a steaks for chrissakes! My PA just spoke to Brian this mawning who knew we'd only be in the city for like, a few ow-uz t'nite! Cuz like, I need my Learjet refueled in Teeta-burrow? I mean, like, we just flew in from Hotel dew Cap. Ever been? I didn't think so. Anyway, we gotta be in Palm Beach by, like, midnight? I mean like, I could *buy this place* and now, like, my driver is double-parked in front of Soho House, like, wade-ing for us? I mean, like, hel-*lo*? Are you kidding me, guy?"

1

"I'm sorry, but we're fully committed," the host deadpanned.

Fully committed? What a peculiar rebuff. Anyway, I watched the display of these poor ladies and thought to myself, "Thank the fine Lord that I have my reservation." Well, actually it was my dinner companion's reservation. She had been given the "secret reservation number" because she happened to chew on a piece of glass there one night.

"We're setting up your table now," he said to us. "It'll be a few minutes. If you'd like to have a drink at the bar, we'll find you when your table is ready." The B-and-T ladies stormed out in a huff.

"Find" was the operative word. The bar was four-deep. We decided to hover by the stand for those few minutes. Just then, a little man with many gold chains and a giraffe-like woman draped over him walked up to the stand. Her hips were just in line with the plugs at the top of his forehead, which she stroked lovingly. He shook the host's hand for a few seconds longer than necessary as he leaned in and introduced himself. One minute later they were escorted to a corner banquette. Our banquette. We were told it would now be another thirty minutes.

PARIS

Ah! Bonjour.

Good day, madame.

Uh, okay, you speak English.

Oui. How can I hewlp you, pleece?

Uh . . . great! I was wondering if I can book a table for two on the twenty-eighth of April—any time after eight P.M. would be preferable.

Non, we are compleetely sold out.

Wow, okay, but that's in two months.

Oui.

Okay, perhaps that Friday, the twenty-ninth?

Non, eet eez not possibul.

The first of May? It's a Tuesday.

Non, eet eez not possibul.

Why is it not possible?

We are very occupé at theez time. Perhaps you can telephone at another time. Au 'voir, madame. (*click*)

So, I tried again.

Bonjour, c'est possible pour un reservation pour le samedi, le vingt-huit d'Avril? J'adore votre chef. Je visite Paris pour le . . . la semaine et j'ai très faim comme une grosse couchon."

(*pause*) Oui.

J'adore le gratinée et les huîtres. Avez-vous voir *La Grande Bouffe*? (*I love outrageous encounters and oysters. Have you seen* The Big Buffet?)

Je ne peux pas supporter ce débile Mastroianni. (*I can't stand Mastroianni.*)

Où est Monsieur Thibault? (*Where is Mr. Thibault?*)

. . . Il n'ya que les minables, les refoulés, et les pourris qui partousent . . . (*. . . Only the pathetic, the repressed, and the rotten have orgies . . .*)

Monsieur Thibault ouvre la fenêtre. *(Mr. Thibault opens the window.)*

...et le film a eu un succès boeuf. Alors...vous parlez très bien le français, madame. *(...and the film was a massive success. So anyway...your French is very good, madame.)*

Merci beaucoup! *(Thank you very much!)*

Et bien, votre reservation? *(So, your reservation?)*

Oui, ce samedi. Deux personnes, à vingt et un heures? *(Yes, this Saturday for two people at nine P.M.?)*

Peut-être. Votre nom? *(Maybe. Your name?)*

Bruni. *(Bruni.)*

Êtes-vous parents? *(Any relation?)*

Non, mes parents ne sont pas ici. *(No, my parents aren't here.)*

Ah—puh! Très charmante. Bien, ce samedi, et combien de personnes? *(You are very charming. Okay then, this Saturday, and how many people?)*

I love the French. But little did I know that *grosse couchon* is slang for "fat whore." I went around saying that expression for a year until someone finally broke it to me. Still, it certainly opened a lot of doors.

LONDON

Hello, this is Suzanne Pirret, and I'd like to make a reservation for the fifteenth of May for four people at nine.

I'm sorry, but we are completely booked.

Okay, well, perhaps that Friday?

I'm sorry, we are completely booked that weekend.

Oh, that's such a shame! My mother is flying in from New York and she was very much looking forward to dining at your restaurant. She's heard so much about it from me.

I'm sorry, we are fully booked.

I've been talking about it forever.

I'm sorry.

Listen, this is a big trip for her. She's very very old.

Yes, I see. I'm very sorry.

But . . . Tom is a friend of mine.

I'm so sorry, madam, but we are completely booked.

But I'm a regular customer and have spent thousands at your restaurant. And I've never stolen anything.

As I said, we are completely booked.

Another time? Six? Early-bird special?

I'm sorry, but all of our reservations have been confirmed at this time.

But I may be bringing, and please keep this quiet, Gwyneth and Chris. Maybe even Madonna.

I don't know what else to tell you, madam.

I'm pregnant.

Congratulations, madam.

And I'm dying.

I'm very sorry, madam.

Listen, if you don't give me a reservation, I will blow up your restaurant . . . with Tom in it.

I do not appreciate your threats, Ms. Pirret. (*Ugh, she remembered my name. Blacklisted forever.*) Now, please, I have told you repeatedly . . . (*Why hasn't she hung up on me yet? It happens to me all the time with Sky, BT, British Gas.*) Now I don't know what else to say to you.

And *I* don't know what else to say to you. (*pause*) Can you please just help me out here? (*silence*) You're not even from here, are you?

No, I'm from Estonia.

Go back to your country!

And you too, Ms. Pirret.

Whatever. (*click*)

I know, rules are rules in London and no one budges, but I just couldn't help myself. Perhaps that's why I still can't buck the system.

LOS ANGELES

Hey, how ya doin'? Can I get a reservation at nine for two people tonight?

Sure, no problem, but, like, make sure you get here on time. Our kitchen closes at, like, nine-fifteen.

Do you know what I love about L.A.? No one eats! (Only sushi, I mean sashimi—no carbs.) You can get a reservation just about anywhere—as long as it's after nine P.M. The whole city shuts down after ten! Hooray for those anorexic-bulimic-carbophobe-yoga-crazed-wheat-grass-drinking fanatics. I LOVE L.A.! (But only to dine out. God help us.)

Sometimes, I'd rather just stay home. Here are a few bistro classics to make for yourself, with no hassle.

BEST STEAK AU POIVRE WITH FRITES

This is my death row dish—all I'd want before my big send-off. The recipe is choreographed so that your fries will be in sync with your steak. Because, if my steak was cold and my fries were soggy, I'd just go straight to the chair. Eat (well) or die, as they say. Or in this case, eat well; then die.

Take out your dry-aged **filet steak** (onglet or pavé are good too). It needs to be at room temperature before you cook it.

Scrub two large **potatoes** well (Maris Piper or Russet are traditionally perfect) and cut them into Mickey D lookalikes. Rinse well in cold water to remove the starch. Place in a pot of cold water with a good pinch of **salt** and bring to a boil. They should be just blanched at this point—careful not to overcook, or they'll fall apart. Drain and plunge immediately into a bowl of icy cold water, spread out on a rack, and refrigerate.

Heat 3 to 4 inches **peanut (groundnut) oil** in a large, deep pan (or medium saucepan) to 250°F (130°C). No thermometer? One tiny drop of water should crackle and sputter gently in the oil.

Now place the blanched, cooled, and *well-dried* potatoes in the hot oil in a single layer. If they're not dry, they'll turn to mush when you fry them. And don't crowd those babies—you may have to do a few batches, depending on how hungry you are. Fry for a few minutes until crisp but still pale. Drain and place back in the fridge to let dry.

Meanwhile, salt both sides of the steak with crushed **Maldon salt** and press some cracked **black and white peppercorns** onto one side until covered. Lift and shake off any excess powder.

Pour 1 to 2 tablespoons **grapeseed oil** into a frying pan and heat till smoking. I mean it should be seriously *hot.* (Note: grapeseed oil has the highest smoke point at 475°F [250°C]. It's also high in anti-oxidants and decreases impotence.) Place your filet in the pan, peppercorn side down. It should sizzle wildly. Turn down the heat just slightly and listen till it's under control. Leave it there. It needs to be left undisturbed to form a deep brown crust. Add a large spoonful of **butter** to the pan, let it bubble up, tip pan to one side, and spoon butter over your filet a few times. You should be able to see a deep brown crust around the edges of the steak. Flip it over, and continue spooning butter over as the steak browns on the other side—a few more minutes. Touch it and press down gently. If you get a slight resistance but it's still quite juicy, it's done (medium-rare). Remove and set aside to rest. Remove the pan from the heat.

Turn up the heat on the fry oil till it's even hotter than before—375°F (190°C). Test a fry. It should brown rather quickly. Place the rest of the fries in the oil. While they're cooking . . .

Pat out the burnt butter from the steak pan with a paper towel. Off the heat, pour in a glug of **brandy or cognac**, return to the heat, and let the alcohol cook off. (I doubt there'll be any bits from the pan to scrape up and use, but that'll be your call.) Add 3 or 4 table-spoons of **veal demi-glace**† **or veal stock** and any drippings from the resting filet and reduce the liquid down a few minutes over high

---

† For veal demi-glace, go to Sources (page 217).

heat. Add a chunk of butter for a little sheen and shake the pan back and forth until melted. Taste it. Season if necessary and add another chunk or two of butter, if you'd like. Keep warm while you . . .

Use a slotted spoon to remove your fries, which should be golden and crispy. Drain on paper towels. Place the steak on a plate, pour the sauce over, and pile up the fries alongside. And for some color and probably the best nourishment of your day, add a small bunch of freshly washed **watercress** alongside and a glass of **Ribero del Duero Unico**, **Vega Sicilia**, or a **Cabernet Franc** from the Collio hills in Friuli. Stunning.

STEAK TARTARE

Alternatively, if you don't feel like cooking the steak . . .

Hand-chop the filet (which should be cold and not at room temperature), mix in some **capers**, finely chopped **fresh flat-leaf parsley**, and a dash of **Worcestershire**, and mound it onto a plate. Use the back of a spoon to lightly press a small indentation in the center to create space for the **quail egg** you'll crack in. Serve with the fries and a few slices of toasted Poilâne.

BEST MAC 'N' CHEESE

Nothing fussy or weird. This is the real deal.

Cook a cup of **elbow macaroni** in boiling salted water with a little oil added. Meanwhile, in another saucepan, make a béchamel: melt a tablespoon of **butter**, whisk in a tablespoon of **flour**, and cook until bubbly. Add a cup of cold **milk** and continue whisking until thickened. Season with **salt**, **white pepper**, a nice pinch of hot **chili powder**, and some chopped **fresh thyme or flat-leaf parsley** (or just a simple grating of fresh nutmeg). Stir in a cup of grated cheese, such as a combo of **white and yellow Cheddar**, or some **parmigiano** and/or **Emmental**—whatever your favorites may be. You have a lot of choices.

Drain the pasta and toss into your béchamel. Spoon into a small casserole dish, sprinkle with toasted **fresh or panko breadcrumbs**, place on a baking sheet, and stick in a 400°F (200°C) oven until golden and bubbly, about 15 minutes or so.

Drink whatever you want.

BEST BRAISED LAMB SHANK

A rustic and hearty caveman-looking dish for when you're craving comfort.

Have your butcher french the bone of a **lamb shank**—or do it yourself.[†] Sprinkle the lamb shank all over with crushed **Maldon salt** and coarsely ground **black pepper**. Coat lightly in flour and shake off the excess.

In hot **olive oil**, sear the shank on all sides. Remove it and wipe out the pan. Over low heat and in a little more oil, sweat a whole thinly sliced small **red onion** and two finely chopped **garlic cloves**, a tablespoon of finely chopped **rosemary**, a little **salt**, and some **cracked black pepper**. Cook slowly until it's soft but not brown. Add half of a bottle of a good **red wine** and 2 tablespoons of **aged balsamic vinegar**. Add the lamb shank, cook for a few minutes, then transfer to an ovenproof saucepan with a lid. If you don't have a lid, foil works (if you happen to own a fancy little Le Creuset, use that). Place in a 300°F (150°C) oven for 2½ to 3 hours, until the meat is falling off the bone. Check every half hour or so and spoon the braising liquid over the lamb. Add more wine (or a dark meat stock), if necessary.

[†] To french the bone: Slice around the bone 2 to 3 inches from the bottom. Scrape away all the flesh so you're left with a clean bone supporting a big hunk of meat.

An hour into the cooking, wash and dry two **potatoes** (or four, see Gnocchi, page 200). Wrap them with foil, prick a few times with a fork, and place in the oven.

When the lamb is done, gently remove and spoon the fat from the top of the liquid. Over high heat, reduce it down for 5 to 10 minutes until slightly thickened and check the seasoning. (If using Le Creuset, you may have to transfer the liquid to another saucepan.) Return the lamb gently to the pot, cover, and keep warm.

Remove the foil from the potatoes, slice them in half, scoop out the insides, and place them in a medium bowl. While they're piping hot, mash up with fork until you can't any longer.

In a small saucepan, heat half a cup of **milk** and/or **cream** and a few tablespoons of **butter** till hot and the butter has melted. Using a wooden spoon, slowly incorporate as much liquid into the potatoes as needed to make them thick and creamy. Add salt and black pepper to taste. Or as an alternative: mash the potatoes well and drizzle in **extra virgin olive oil**. Beat well, then season well.

Spoon the mash onto a plate, top with the lamb shank, and spoon the sauce on top.

We need something rich and intense here with a good acidity and a rich flavor. Try a **Côte-Rôtie** or **St. Joseph** from the Northern Rhône. Or a **Gigondas**.

BEST CHICKEN POT PIE

Just like Mom used to heat up.

PASTRY

Combine ¾ cup (105g) **flour** with a pinch of **salt** in a bowl. Cut 4 tablespoons (60g) of cold **butter** into tiny cubes and work into the flour with your hands until the mixture is coarse and crumbly. Beat an **egg** in a separate bowl and add half of it to the flour and mix in until the dough just comes together. If it's still crumbly, add a few drops of ice cold water. Set the remainder of the egg aside for the pastry later.

That's really it. If you overwork it, your pastry will be tough. Shape it into a ball, flatten it down to an inch, wrap loosely in plastic, and let rest in the fridge while you prepare the . . .

FILLING

    potato—one medium, peeled and quartered

    pearl onions—four or five, peeled

    baby carrots—a few, peeled

    mushrooms—a bunch of tiny enoki tips or some other interesting seasonal variety

    peas—2 to 3 tablespoons of fresh or frozen

    fresh tarragon—finely chopped

Cook the potato in boiling salted water until a knife runs easily through it. Remove and set aside. Rinse out the pot. Add the onions and cover with water. Bring to a boil and simmer gently until you can stick a paring knife into one, lift the knife straight up, and the onion slides down the blade easily. Remove, reserving the water. Add the carrots and cook gently until just done. Drain, discarding the water, cut into small cubes, and set aside. Cut the potato into small cubes and set aside with the vegetables.

Rinse the pot well, dry it, and return it to the heat. Add a little **oil**, add the mushrooms, and cook till just brown. Season with salt and **pepper** and add to the other vegetables.

Lightly pound a **chicken breast** to a uniform thickness. Place it in a small frying pan and cover with **chicken stock**, water, or even white wine if you're drinking it at the moment, a few cloves of smashed **garlic**, a few **black peppercorns**, and a few sprigs of **fresh tarragon**. If you have a **lemon**, add a large peel. Bring to a very gentle simmer and poach until it's just cooked through. Remove and keep warm. Discard the cooking liquid.

To make the béchamel: in a saucepan, melt about a tablespoon of butter. Whisk in a tablespoon of flour and let cook till it's bubbly and just beginning to brown. Pour in about a cup of chicken stock and whisk into the roux until it begins to thicken. Lower the heat, add a few spoonfuls of **milk or cream**, and continue whisking vigorously until it thickens to the consistency of cream of chicken soup. Remove from the heat and season with **Maldon salt** and **white pepper**.

Cut the chicken into small cubes. Stir into the sauce with all the vegetables. Add the tarragon and season to taste.

(I swear we're almost done.) Take out your pastry and slice off two-thirds for the bottom crust and one-third for the top. Roll out the bottom to fit inside a mold, plus an inch or two for overhang (I've used a medium soufflé dish or a small deep oval ceramic). Improvise. Spoon in the filling. Roll out the top pastry and place on top. Crimp the bottom and the top of the pastry together. Brush with the remaining beaten egg. Use the tip of a knife to cut a few one-inch steam vents in top crust. Place on a baking sheet and bake in a 350°F (180°C) oven until golden and bubbly, 20 to 30 minutes.

I like this with a mellow white wine, such as a **Carneros Chardonnay**.

BEST DUCK CONFIT

Start this on a Friday. Throw in the oven on Saturday. Eat blissfully on Sunday. And don't be fooled, the total prep time is about fifteen minutes. The rest has very little to do with you.

With a mortar and pestle, grind down ¼ cup of **Maldon salt**, a few **black peppercorns**, a tablespoon or two of chopped **fresh flat-leaf parsley**, and a heaping teaspoon of chopped **fresh thyme**. Blend well.

Trim the extra fat from four **duck legs** (keep a small overhang of fat—it will shrink back when cooking), slightly french the bone (see page 12) for a little elegance, and rub the salt mixture all over each leg. Place flesh side down in a dish, cover, and refrigerate for no more than 24 hours, or they'll be too salty.

Rinse the legs well with cold water and dry them with paper towels. Place in a baking dish and cover completely with **duck or goose fat**—about two 7-ounce containers (or one 350g tin) per leg, but have a few extra containers just in case. Cover with lid (or foil) and cook slowly in oven at 190°F (90°C) until ridiculously tender—up to 10 hours. Let cool in the fat.

Transfer the legs (without the fat) to a casserole dish, large jar, or earthenware pot, seal tightly, and refrigerate. Meanwhile, strain the fat and refrigerate it separately in an airtight container or a large bowl that has been securely wrapped. Your aim is to get rid of the meat jelly at the bottom so that you can store the duck for several months—you may not want duck confit four times in the next two weeks, y'know? So, when the fat solidifies, spoon it out and discard the gelatinized duck juices that have settled at the bottom. Now re-melt the fat and pour it over the duck. The confit will now last a few months in your fridge. Sometimes I just like the look of having a jar of duck confit in an otherwise empty refrigerator. It's an aesthetic thing.

When you want to eat, let the container sit out until the fat is slightly softened, then gently scoop out a leg. Pan-fry skin side down in a hot and smoking oil-free pan, and let it sizzle like crazy for several minutes, until it's golden brown and the skin is quite hard and crispy. Open your windows. Flip over, turn the heat down, and cook for several minutes until heated through. Remove.

At this point, toss in some vegetables, such as **baby carrots** and 2- to 3-inch slices of **baby leeks**, and gently braise in the duck fat till they begin to brown. Remove from the heat and slowly add a few tablespoons of water or stock, a drizzle of **aged balsamic**, and a **star anise**. Return to low heat and continue cooking very slowly until the vegetables become tender and slightly caramelized. Squeeze in a spoonful of fresh **lemon juice**. Remove from heat and stir in some chopped **fresh flat-leaf parsley** (or tarragon). Season with a little **black pepper**. Pile the vegetables on a plate and place the duck confit on top.

Great with a Pinot Noir such as **Côtes de Nuits** from Burgundy or a **Fixin** (which isn't as pricy). But the ideal wine would be a **Chambertin** or a **Musigny**.

While your duck confit is cooking, your oven will be on for ten hours, so get the most out of it—you eco-friendly, energy-efficient person, you.

ROAST GARLIC: Drizzle a few heads of garlic with olive oil, wrap them in foil, and roast for an hour, or until soft. Leave in their skins and store in an airtight container. Squeeze out to use in pastas, aiolis, salad dressings . . . garlic mania!

ROAST NUTS on a sheet for 10 minutes, or until golden—set the timer on your BlackBerry.

DRY FRESH CHILES: Spread on a baking sheet and let dry out in the oven for a few hours. Careful not to burn. Store in a mason jar and crush between your fingers before using.

DRY SLICED FRUIT: Perhaps in another lifetime. Far too Martha Stewart for me.

BEST CRAB CAKES

I tried all types of fillers here—oyster crackers soaked in cream, mashed potatoes, fresh breadcrumbs, eggs, flour—but no! They all disguised the great taste of the almighty crab. You pay enough for it, why hide it? Delicate morsels of sweet succulent crab and a lemony tartar sauce. There you go.

Sweat a finely chopped small **shallot** (a tablespoon) in some **butter**. Add a finely minced small **jalapeño pepper** (a teaspoon) and cook for a minute or two. Remove from the heat. Now, before adding 1½ to 2 cups of **fresh lump crabmeat**, it is imperative that you sift through it carefully with your hands and remove any sharp objects, shells, bones, cartilage—anything. They'll most likely be there, and to have to continuously pull them from your mouth later is a total drag. Add some finely chopped **fresh dill, cilantro, or flat-leaf parsley, sea salt**, and **black pepper**. Whisk an unused **egg white** (from the tartar sauce you'll be making to accompany this—see Best Fish & Chips, page 24) till it's frothy and add just enough to moisten the crab. Mix in a small spoonful of **cornstarch (cornflour)**, or just enough so that you can scoop up a portion of crab mixture into your hands and shape it into a thick patty—you should get about three. They'll be fragile, so keep them in the fridge till ready to use, at which point you can make that tartar sauce and a big green salad.

Gently pat the crab cakes into a plate of **panko breadcrumbs**, shake off any excess, and gently pan-fry them in a few tablespoons of hot **olive or peanut (groundnut) oil**—about ¼ inch deep—until deep golden brown on each side.

I would have given you a recipe for a fresh coleslaw to go alongside—the traditional combo—but cabbage heads are too big and usually just sit and rot in my refrigerator, so forget about it.

New World wines are the norm here in London and I've become a loyal fan of several, two in particular: a **Margaret River Sauvignon Blanc** from Australia, such as **Cloudy Bay**, or a **Marlborough SB** from New Zealand, such as **Craggy Range**. Bright summery fruits that never let me down.

BEST PORK CHOPS AND APPLESAUCE

Many people think pork needs to be cooked for seventeen hours—long enough to ensure you won't get trichinosis. This may have been necessary when pigs' diets consisted of garbage gnawed at by infected rodents. Nice. But since that was banned and you know how your pigs are being raised, you're okay. This chop is truly succulent and best cooked medium-rare to medium (137°F/58°C, just in case you're checking).

Have your butcher cut you **a double-thick-cut pork chop on the bone** (about 2 inches thick) and trim most of the fat off. And ask him how the pigs were raised.

Rinse and dry the chop and place it in a bowl. Cover with **milk**, a squeeze of **lemon**, two smashed **garlic cloves**, two sprigs of **fresh thyme**, and a little **olive oil**. Cover and refrigerate for an hour or two, or even better, overnight.

Heat the oven to 400°F (200°C). Drain the pork, then **salt** and **pepper** each side well. Sear in hot olive oil all over till brown, then add a few fresh smashed garlic cloves and a few sprigs of fresh thyme to the pan. Transfer to the oven and roast for about 15 to 20 minutes, till it's pale pink and juicy, as it should be. Let rest for 10 minutes.

Meanwhile, wash and roughly dice two seasonal **apples**, unpeeled, of your choice. If they're quite small, use three. Melt a tablespoon of **butter** in a pan and add the apples, half a **cinnamon stick**, a tiny pinch of ground **cloves**, and a pinch of **Maldon salt**. Cook down a bit and add a glug of **Calvados**. Let cook gently and mash down with a fork. Taste. You may want to add a little honey and/or lemon juice. Continue cooking until the apples are soft and all the liquid has been absorbed. Season with black pepper, as desired.

Spoon any jus from the pan onto the pork chop, drizzle on a little **extra virgin olive oil**, and serve with the warm applesauce and a **German Riesling**. Make sure you go into your wine shop and say, "I'm looking for a richer take of a **Spätlese** from the Middle Mosel, like a **Wehlener Sonnenuhr**." Then snub him if you don't see the words "Joh," "Jos," or "Prüm" (the best producers) on any of his labels.

BEST FISH & CHIPS

Britain's national dish. I'm definitely a convert. Posh street food at its best.

For the chips, follow the recipe from Best Steak au Poivre with Frites, page 8, only cut them into thick, fat chips of uniform size so they all cook equally. After the chips have been cooked twice, come back to this page.

You'll need a fillet or two of a preferably non-endangered local **white fish** (go to www.fishonline.org for updates). At the moment, I'm using wild red snapper, gurnard, and pollock here in ol' Blighty. We'll see about next year.

Pour ¼ cup (60ml) of your favorite **lager beer** in a bowl. Drink the rest. Whisk in ⅓ cup (45g) **flour** and half a teaspoon **baking powder**. Add half a teaspoon **honey** and let sit for about 10 to 15 minutes, just enough time to prepare your tartar sauce. See the recipe below.

Heat the peanut oil from the fries till a drop of fish batter browns fairly quickly. I always use the back burner when deep-frying—for safety's sake. Drinking and frying? Careful now, my love. Regarding the fillet, the traditional British way to cook it is with its skin on—your choice. Season both sides of your fillet with crushed **sea salt** and **white pepper**, then lightly coat in flour and shake off the excess. Dredge in the batter. Lift out with a large spoon—it'll be really thick—and sslllowwwly place in the oil, drizzling more of the batter over the fish. Again, try not to have an intimate relationship with your fish while it's cooking. Give it some space, or it just might spit at you. Fry until deep golden brown—it should take no longer than 5 to 8 minutes for a medium piece of fish. Remove and drain on paper towels. Then, using the same oil, follow up with the second frying of the chips, which should only take a few minutes. Pile the fish and chips together in a paper cone made from Page 3 of the *Sun* or from Page Six of the *New York Post* (same stuff, no tits) and dunk into **tartar sauce or ketchup**, or pour on some **malt vinegar**.

Guinness anyone?

TARTAR SAUCE

Whisk together an **egg yolk**, a squeeze of fresh **lemon juice**, and a dash of **white wine vinegar**. You want the total volume to be no more than 1 or 2 tablespoons, so adjust accordingly—otherwise you'll be making tartar sauce for a family of twelve. While whisking, very slowly drizzle in about half a cup **grapeseed oil**—it's lighter than olive—or half of each, in a long steady stream until thick. Stir in finely chopped **sweet pickles**, **capers**, a bit of a minced **shallot**, and some finely chopped **fresh flat-leaf parsley**. Season with salt and pepper.

THE CRUEL REVENGE OF GENERAL TSAO

HOW TO MAKE TAKE-OUT

Listen, is this the lobster man? Good. Send us up some lobster with drawn butter and two scrambled eggs and four toasted bialys with cream cheese and some Pepsi-Cola and a bottle of tequila with plenty of lemon. You got that? Good.

—SAM SHEPARD, *Cowboy Mouth*

It was 1988 and my apartment building on West 80th Street in Manhattan had just made the cover of *Newsweek*. It was featured as the last remaining crack building on the Upper West Side. (It was rent-stabilized, what can I say?) There was a picture of a person sitting on the front stoop. She had large breasts and a long beard, and was nicknamed Wilda Beast. Her friends loved to while away the hours on that front stoop, which during the day would be littered with chicken wing bones and yellow styrofoam containers. In the morning, I'd crunch over their crack vials. In the evening, I stayed indoors. Just as they loved their take-out, I loved mine: it meant making one less venture past them. I let the delivery guys do that.

27

Back in those days, take-out was different. A typical evening generally involved a phone call like this:

Hi. I just found a cigarette butt in my General Tsao's Chicken.

Happens. Our chefs very busy.

I want my money back.

(*He snickers.*)

You think it's funny?

(*Snickers again.*)

So you think this is funny. Well, you listen to me, buster. You won't be laughing when I report your filthy establishment to the Board of Health.

You the lady who want white meat?

Uh, yes.

You get your white meat?

Uh, yes. And a lot more. (*I couldn't believe I was having this conversation.*)

You smoka?

Eh . . . yy . . . No! I quit yesterday.

You smoka then. Maybe it your butt.

I don't smoke! And not while I'm eating!

Have some compassion.

Compassion my ass, bring me my money back. Now.

Okay.

And then he'd hang up.

I love Chinese. It's cheap, easy, and arrives fast. Kind of like that late-night booty call you always wish for. On this occasion, it was late and I was ravenous. I phoned my Chinese place on Broadway and gave my usual order. Because I was a regular customer, I had some clout and could skip the address details. Four minutes later, my buzzer rang, the delivery guy appeared, and we made our exchange. Unfortunately for him, it was pissing down rain, but he still managed to keep my dinner dry. I tipped him two bucks and thanked him.

As I unpacked the white origami boxes, I instantly perked up: piping hot grilled pork dumplings with a simple dipping sauce of Chinese vinegar, soy sauce, and a scattering of chopped chives; a greasy but very tasty General Tsao's Chicken (white meat only) with an assortment of fresh multicolored vegetables cut into cool shapes and sizes; and Cold Sesame Noodles packed down so tightly they could feed a family of four. I usually saved this for breakfast.

I devoured the dumplings over my kitchen sink. Then curled up in bed with the Tsao's, turned on a commercial every-five-minutes Turner Classic Movie, and dug in with chopsticks. Life was good. Until I bit down into something oddly spongy. The cigarette butt was sautéed in soy sauce, deeply bronzed, and perfectly intact. I could still clearly read the "Merit Ultra Lights" stamp on it.

I might have cut the chef some slack if it had been a Marlboro Red. I would have had a little empathy for the nicotine-ravaged slave in the kitchen cranking out four hundred orders of General Tsao's on a Sunday night. But in this case, he could have held out until his break. Pussy.

These are the recipes I like to make when I'm lazy, far away from home.

CHINESE
GENERAL TSAO'S CHICKEN

For the chicken: cube two **chicken breasts**, place in a bowl, and mix in one or two spoonfuls of **soy sauce** and a dash of **white pepper**. Stir in a beaten **egg** and sprinkle in enough **cornstarch (cornflour)** so it all clumps together and is quite pastelike. Add a drizzle of **olive oil** to separate the chicken cubes. Set aside.

For the sauce: mix a spoonful of cornstarch and half that amount of hot water till a nice paste forms. Add a small spoon each of minced **garlic**, grated **fresh ginger**, **sugar**, and **white wine vinegar**. Stir in half to ¾ cup hot **chicken stock** and mix till incorporated. Taste (yes, taste) and adjust to your liking. Set aside.

Now heat half an inch of **peanut oil** in a frying pan until hot—test one piece of chicken. When it begins to brown, add the rest and cook in one layer—don't crowd—until golden and crispy. Set aside to drain.

Remove the oil from the pan and wipe clean with paper towels. Add a little peanut oil again and stir-fry a few thinly sliced **scallions** and a finely minced **red chile pepper** (or a pinch or two of crushed red chile flakes). Add the sauce to the pan until it thickens, stir in the chicken, and heat it all through.

Serve over *rice:* in a saucepan, bring water and rice of choice in 2:1 ratio to a boil. Cover and simmer over low heat until done. Add a pinch of salt.

Also, you can steam some **broccoli** on the side, double the sauce recipe, and mix it in with the chicken.

All the Chinese, Thai, and Indian dishes can happily be paired with **German Rieslings**—one of the great grapes of the world. Colum Sheehan, our sommelier here, has remarked that most people assume these wines are too sweet and wants to reinforce the fact that you should never judge based on a first impression. He says that at *first*, you get hit with the sweet fruit. But this is a must for spicy foods because the sweetness provides a cushion for the spice. Hold your judgment for a few seconds and let the experience take place. The acidity then comes through and cleanses the sweetness, leaving the mouth feeling very fresh and dry. Without that acidity, the wine would be flabby and just fall apart. The wines are also more moderate in their alcohol content—having just 10 percent. Any wine with a higher alcohol content combined with the heat from the spices will clash, which would be such a disappointment after a great cooking effort.

COLD SESAME NOODLES

Best in the morning, noon, night, and middle of the night.

Whisk together about a tablespoon each of **sesame oil**, **Chinese rice vinegar**, **Chinese sesame paste**, and **smooth peanut butter**; half a tablespoon each of **fresh and finely grated ginger** and **sugar** (dissolved in a tablespoon of hot water); and half a teaspoon each of **chili paste** and **minced garlic.**

Add one or two dashes of **soy sauce** and a squeeze of **fresh lime juice** to taste.

Toss with a good portion of **fresh Chinese egg noodles**, cooked al dente and mixed with a little **sesame oil** so that they don't clump together. Garnish with peeled, seeded, and julienned **cucumber** and some roasted and chopped **peanuts**.

Eat with chopsticks.

CRISPY DUCK WITH
WARM FRESH PLUM SAUCE

Okay, time to break out your duck confit (see Best Duck Confit, page 17).

Bring your jar of **duck confit** to room temperature.

Meanwhile, pit four or five small **red plums** (or other seasonal variety) and chop coarsely. Place in a saucepan with a cup of **water**, half a cup (100g) of **sugar**, a **cinnamon stick** snapped in half, a small pinch of **cloves**, a **star anise**, four cracked **Szechuan peppercorns**, a little **fresh ginger**, a dash of **fish sauce**, and a squeeze of **fresh lime juice**. Bring to a boil, then lower the heat and reduce gently until thick. Press through a sieve and set aside.

Julienne a **cucumber**, discarding the seeds, and three or four trimmed **scallions** so the batons are roughly equal in size (about 3 inches long and half an inch wide).

Gently scoop a duck leg from the fat and wipe off the excess. Put the jar back in the fridge. The more fat you wipe off now, the less splatter you'll have as you're searing it. Heat a frying pan until smoking and add the duck, skin side down. Turn down the heat slightly until it's under control. Cook until the skin is a deep golden brown and seriously crispy—a good 5 minutes. Turn over and cook for another 3 to 5 minutes, until heated through. Remove and drain on paper towels. Shred the meat and skin roughly.

Steam a few **Chinese pancakes**. I do not own—and probably never will—a basket steamer for this kind of stuff. Here is a make-shift alternative: Immerse a clean tea towel in steaming hot water and wring it out well. Lay it flat, stack a few pancakes in the center, and fold up the towel. Place on a baking sheet and warm in a 200°F (100°C) oven for about 10 minutes.

Lay out a pancake, spread on the sauce, layer on the vegs and duck, and roll up.

INDIAN

COCONUT FISH CURRY

A traditional fresh curry for one person is just too much work—too many ingredients—and the prepared curries just don't compare, so I bagged the idea. But this humble curry dish does the trick for me. It's very delicate, light, and wispy and best served with rice (page 30).

Rub a little **sea salt** and **turmeric** on both sides of a fresh **sea bass** fillet. Heat a little **grapeseed oil** in a pan and sweat a small handful of finely sliced **onions**, a minced **garlic clove**, a minced small **green chile**, and several **curry leaves** until transluscent and soft. Add half a cup (125ml) **coconut milk** and a good teaspoon of **turmeric** and gently simmer.

Meanwhile, pan-fry several curry leaves in a little grapeseed oil till crisp and set aside. In the same pan, roast the fillet, skin side down, until crispy. Turn over and cook for a few more minutes. The fillet should be slightly firm but give a little. Remove from the pan immediately. Spoon the sauce onto the plate. Place the fillet on top and garnish with chopped **fresh cilantro** and the crispy curry leaves.

HOME-STYLE YELLOW SPLIT PEAS

No soaking of beans required for this sassy little number.

In a saucepan, sauté a teaspoon of minced **garlic** in olive oil until light brown and stir in a half to one teaspoon of hot **red chile powder.** Add a cup of water, a half cup (110g) **yellow split peas**, two pinches of **turmeric**, and a nice pinch of **Maldon salt** and gently simmer, uncovered, for 20 minutes. Add more water if the lentils begin sticking to the bottom. Add a roughly chopped **tomato** and continue cooking gently until soft, another 10 to 15 minutes. Garnish with chopped **fresh cilantro**.

HOMEMADE NAAN BREAD

Make this on the spot—or bang this out before you go to sleep and keep in fridge to use in the next day or two. It is excellent—even without a tandoori oven.

Sift together 1¼ cups (175g) **self-raising (self-rising) flour**, a pinch of **sugar**, two pinches of **salt**, and a teaspoon of **baking powder**. In another bowl, whisk together 3 tablespoons (32ml) each of water and **milk** and a small beaten **egg**. Combine with the dry ingredients until mixed well. Knead on a floured counter for 5 to 10 minutes or until smooth and elastic. Place in a bowl, cover with plastic, and refrigerate for a few hours or overnight.

Cut the dough into thirds. On a lightly floured board or counter, flatten or roll the balls into ¼-inch-thick disks (very thin). You can keep them plain or sprinkle with toasted **cumin seeds**. Heat a frying pan and add a little **olive oil**. Place a disk in the pan and let it bubble up. Flip it over and brown the other side. Repeat.

VARIATIONS

When the dough has been flattened into a disk, try either combo:
- finely chopped **garlic** and **extra virgin olive oil**
- desiccated **coconut**, **raisins** (macerate by plumping in hot

water for 5 minutes), and a little **palm sugar**, mixed into a thick paste

Spread the mixture on one end of the dough, fold the opposite end over, and gently flatten or roll out the dough again. Proceed with the frying.

THAI

JASMIN'S PAD THAI

Jasmin is a piece of work. Her single-word name only enhances her celebrity status. She's the chef/proprietor of her eponymous quintessential beach hut restaurant on the northern tip of Koh Phi Phi in Thailand. A tall, sexy native with long jet black hair and flowing silk dresses, she's as sharp as a razor blade and intimidating as hell. If you ask her a question, she stops, squints her eyes dubiously, and raises an eyebrow. All I can say is . . . you don't fuck with Jasmin. She's the Queen Bee here. Her worker bees are the little barefoot gypsy kids who live on the beach, the happiest kids I've ever seen. They take her orders, serve her food, and assist her in effortlessly knocking out the freshest and most delicious Thai dishes around—her clientele buzzes in from every surrounding island. "Just bring us whatever you'd like" (I try to skip the questions). I'll kick back with a Singha and watch those iconic longtail boats pull up with ice crates of screamingly fresh local fish—and I'm eating perfectly executed delicacies fifteen minutes later. Here's a woman who is truly about abundance, joie de vivre, and a spirit so vibrant that it inspires everyone. A true domestic goddess. She graciously taught me this classic in her (outdoor) kitchen on the beach.

red onion—2 tablespoons, finely chopped

peanut or olive oil—a dash

shrimp (deveined), or **calamari** (cleaned and sliced), or **chicken or pork** (thinly sliced)

an egg

thai rice noodles—a small handful

chicken stock or water—half a cup (max)

fish sauce—four to five glugs

tamarind sauce[‡]—a heaping tablespoon

palm sugar or unrefined caster sugar—half tablespoon

crushed red chile flakes—a pinch or two

bean sprouts—a handful

scallions—three or four, cut into 3-inch sticks

raw cashews—2 to 3 tablespoons, coarsely chopped

fresh lime wedges and **cucumber slices**—for garnish

Get your mise completely ready to go, because this dish only takes about 5 minutes to cook.

In a wok (of course you can use a frying pan, but it's just not the same; even those cheap stainless steel ones work better than a pan), fry the red onion in a little peanut or olive oil. Add the shrimp (or calamari, chicken, or pork). Cook for a minute. They'll continue

---

[‡]Tamarind sauce—of course you can buy this already prepared, but it's an entirely different sauce when it's fresh: place a small handful (about 2 to 3 tablespoons) of dried, vacu-packed tamarind nuggets in a bowl and cover with very hot water for about 5 to 10 minutes to soften. Use your hands to squish the nuggets until the water becomes really thick and gloopy. You'll notice your hands getting really soft, so spread a good amount of it all over your arms and face. Great for the skin. Anyway, using a rubber spatula, rub the sauce through a strainer, leaving the pits behind. Store the sauce in an airtight mason jar (keeps about a week). Rinse off your arms and face.

cooking, so don't worry too much if they're still slightly opaque, and move them over to the side. Make a well in the center. Crack the egg in there and scramble with a fork till cooked. Push over to the side along with the shrimp.

Break the noodles in half (unless your wok is the huge industrial size), and add to the center with about ¼ cup of the stock, the fish sauce, tamarind sauce, palm sugar (dissolve it in a little hot water if too thick), and red chile flakes. Mix well into the noodles, leaving the shrimp and scrambled egg off to the side.

Cook the noodles in the sauce for a few minutes, stirring lightly to ensure that they don't clump together. The noodles should be just softened—you want them nice and chewy. Taste and adjust the seasoning—and add more stock if necessary.

Now add the bean sprouts and the scallions, stir everything together, and heat it through. Immediately turn onto large plate and top with the chopped cashews. Garnish with lime and cucumber slices.

You now just need a pair of chopsticks and an ice cold **Singha**.

TOM YUM KUNG SOUP

Forget chicken soup for a cold. This will kill anything you have lurking in your system.

In a pot, combine 2 cups fresh **chicken stock**, two smashed **garlic cloves**, three julienned **kaffir lime leaves**, a few slices of fresh or dried **galangal**, a dash of **fish sauce**, two **lemongrass** stalks—bashed slightly and cut into one-inch slices—a few sliced **oyster mushrooms**, and the juice from half a **fresh lime.** Bring to a boil and simmer gently for a few minutes. Add six to eight peeled and deveined **fresh shrimp** and cook until pink—a few minutes.

Mix a little **lime juice** and some **roasted chili paste** together and place in a large soup bowl. Pour in the soup and garnish with **fresh cilantro** leaves.

GRILLED LAMB CHOPS WITH LEMONGRASS

You can make this all year round, and depending on your choice of lamb, you'll have different results each time. If using a small rack, it'll be sweet and delicate; with loin chops, hearty and rustic. If you try the latter, be sure to coat both sides with the lemongrass paste and skip the tamarind sauce on the side—it won't be necessary. Also great in the summer on a grill.

Finely chop a few **red chiles** according to taste: 1 = mild; 2 = a bit fiery; 3 or more = an interesting evening of oral sex. Who said you were alone *after* dinner? Finely chop two to three **lemongrass** stalks[†] and a small **shallot**. Using a mortar and pestle, grind it all together with a tablespoon or two of **olive oil** and the same amount of **palm sugar** (white or brown sugar works too), and the juice from a freshly squeezed **lime** until a nice chunky paste forms.

For the lamb, go with a small rack of about four or five chops (for new season spring lamb, the chops are very tiny and lean—barely two bites each—so it depends on how hungry you are). Season all over with **Maldon salt** and **cracked black pepper**. Generously spread the lemongrass paste on top, cover, and let sit out at room temperature for an hour.

Meanwhile, using that **tamarind sauce** you have handy (see

[†] What to do with those extra stalks before they rot? See page 201.

Jasmin's Pad Thai, page 39), heat several tablespoons with a few dashes of **fish sauce** and 1 or 2 teaspoons of **palm sugar**. Adjust the taste to your liking.

Broil the lamb rack about 8 inches from the heat, bone side up first, until it starts to brown and crisp, then flip it over to the meat side, and broil for another few minutes. Bring the oven rack up and finish off the lamb directly below the heat for the last few minutes. You really want to brown the lemongrass—the sweet and crispy marinade tastes delicious this way. Remove and let the lamb rest for several minutes before slicing. Serve with tamarind sauce on the side and lots of creamy **coconut rice**: use jasmine rice in a ratio of 2:1 coconut milk to rice. Add a pinch of salt. Cook gently, uncovered, stirring until tender, as you would a risotto. Continue adding water, if necessary, to keep it from sticking, and it'll cook perfectly into a delicious accompaniment.

FAST FOOD
PIZZA MARGHERITA (NOT DOMINO'S)

My first memory of eating pizza was right outside the original Patsy's in East Harlem, New York. It was the 1970s, long before Clinton moved his entourage up there and deemed the neighborhood "safe." My dad would park the station wagon out front. Although it was his 'hood, where he had grown up, he still made us buckle our seat belts and lock the car doors. There'd always be a few dubious-looking fellas lurking about. He'd give them a quick nod and disappear through the doors. Then we'd all wait in silence. After what seemed like hours, he'd carry out a box of steaming hot pizza straight from the coal-fired oven, one time balanced on top of a new twelve-inch TV. We'd devour the pizza immediately. The car windows fogged up and condensation dripped down, but my dad still insisted it was far too dangerous to open them.

DOUGH

Add half a package **dry yeast** (1 teaspoon) to 2/3 cup (175ml) warm water and let sit for 5 minutes, or until the yeast has dissolved. Stir in half a tablespoon **honey** and a tablespoon of **olive oil**.

Mix 1½ cups (210g) **00 flour** (don't even try to substitute all-purpose—it doesn't make the cut) and a good pinch of crushed **sea**

salt in a bowl and make a well in the center. Add the liquid ingredients and mix with a wooden spoon or your hands until a dough forms. Turn onto lightly floured counter and begin to knead. Knead it. Knead that sweet piece of dough with all the love you can muster, just like they did in twelfth-century Napoli, until it's soft, stretchy, elastic, and aerated. You're developing the gluten—if you don't, it'll just taste like shortcrust pastry—so give it a good 10 to 15 minutes. The dough should be perfectly smooth and plump (I'll try to refrain from clichéd metaphors here). Place in a bowl, cover with plastic wrap, and keep in a warm place until it doubles in size—an hour should be enough.

Punch the dough down and flatten it into a disk. If you're starved, make the whole thing now or, if not, freeze half for future use (lasts up to three months). One half will make you a pizza about 8 by 12 inches, so you decide. Throw the dough back and forth between your hands to stretch and pull it into a nice thin sheet. Definitely throw it up in the air and spin it around a few times. Then bring it back down to the counter and press together the holes you've just made. But keep it as thin as possible. (Or if you'd like, just use a rolling pin.)

You now have a few options: I prefer to honor the Associazione Verace Pizza Napoletana (True Neapolitan Pizza Association). Sort of. Onto a rectangular baking sheet (no, I don't own a pizza stone), throw down the dough—misshapen and perfectly imperfect is ideal. Scoop out a few **San Marzano tomatoes** from a can that you have sourced, crush them lightly, and spoon them all over the pizza (without the liquid), leaving an inch border around the crust. Another excellent can of peeled, seeded, and crushed tomatoes will also do.

Sort of. Sprinkle with **sea salt** and **cracked black pepper**. Scatter over small mounds of the freshest **buffalo mozzarella** you can find. Place on the lowest rack in a preheated hot hot *hot* oven (500°F+) and bake till brown and bubbly (check after 5 minutes). Serve with a drizzle of your best **extra virgin olive oil** and torn **fresh basil leaves**. (Although Da Michele in Naples only uses a single basil leaf.) The pizza police would not entirely approve of mine, but it's still darn good.

Alternatively: Heat a little olive oil in an ovenproof frying pan and place it in a circle of dough to fit. Cook on the stovetop until bubbly and brown. Flip onto the other side and lower the heat slightly. Place your toppings and cheese(s) of choice on top and place under the broiler until melted and bubbly. It'll be puffy and have a whole different taste. Not my fave, but you may like it.

As you know, you can make this as complicated as you want. Make a tomato sauce ahead with chopped fresh tomatoes—or a can of tomatoes—roasted garlic, fresh herbs (oregano, thyme, rosemary, and so on), or those numerous other toppings or bastardizations of toppings you may like. No one else cares.

Try a **Lambrusco** or **Gragnano**—a local wine south of Naples. Or a white wine such as **Greco di Tufo**—another local wine from the Irpinia hills inland from Naples.

But let's not get too precious, it's pizza. How about a **beer**?

FRIED CHICKEN WITH BUTTERMILK BISCUITS (NOT KFC'S)

I have long been fascinated by the late chef Edna Lewis. The fact that she was still banging out dinner after dinner well into her seventies (with her partner, chef Scott Peacock) makes her a legend to behold. This version is inspired by her recipe. One secret is the brine—which is a classic way of tenderizing meat. The transformation astoundingly melts in your mouth. You have to approach the effort involved like this:

One day, when you're doing nothing, take a cup of **kosher salt** and dissolve it in a gallon of boiling hot water. If you have some **herbs** (parsley, thyme, rosemary, the odd bay leaf), add them along with a few smashed **garlic cloves** and some **peppercorns**, but it's not absolutely necessary in this case. Put it aside somewhere to cool. Continue with your social networking sites.

The next day—or even the next week—buy the absolute best quality and freshest **whole chicken** you can afford. Cut into ten parts like this: wash it, clean out the cavity, and dry it. Flip it over so the back is facing up. Cut off the yellow oil gland at the chicken's bum. Cut around one leg, careful not to miss out on the *solilesse.*[†] Repeat on

---

[†] *Solilesse*—a French term meaning "the idiot forgot it." It's the "oyster" of the chicken, located on each side of the very lowest and outermost part of the back. Think of them as those

the other side. Slice through the joints in the middle of each leg to cut in two. Set aside. Now cut straight through the chicken, down the middle, so you're left with the breasts and the wings intact. Cut off the wings and set aside. Hack the breasts in two—with the ribs on—and set aside. Keep the bones for stock, or discard.

And, of course, you can always have your butcher do this for you.

Place the ten pieces in a large bowl, wash them well with cold water, and drain. Pour your cooled brine over the chicken and place the bowl in the fridge for 8 to 12 hours (if you're a forgetful person, just use half the amount of salt in the brine, and the brining process can continue for up to 24 hours).

The following day: Before you head out for the evening, drain and rinse the chicken, then place it back into the bowl. Cover with **milk** and squeeze in the juice of a whole **lemon**. Place back in the fridge again for up to 12 hours.

The very last day: Perhaps it's a Sunday and it's the late afternoon, and you're starved, hungover, and can't be bothered to go outside and get some food. You have your chicken!—the perfect cure-all. Drain, take as many pieces as you'd like to eat (freeze the rest), and coat them in **flour** mixed with a little **cornstarch** (ratio= a cup of flour to a tablespoon of cornstarch), **black pepper**, and if you'd like, a dash of hot **chili powder**.

---

two little pouches that protrude over the back of your far too low-rise jeans. The idiot forgot to cut out enough denim for your oysters. Anyway, those tiny soft pouches of meat are extremely tender and succulent. Probably not as noticeable in fried chicken, but just some food for thought.

Deep-fry in a few inches of hot **peanut (groundnut) oil**. (First test with a pinch of flour—if it browns in a second, you're okay.) If I'm doing a small batch (two or three pieces), I'll use a medium saucepan with high sides and 3 to 4 inches of oil. Works great. Fry the chicken for 5 to 8 minutes for small pieces; double that for larger ones. (When pricked with a fork, the juices must run clear.) Drain and sprinkle with a smidgen of **Maldon salt**. Use the leftover oil for your Prius.

Eat with **BUTTERMILK BISCUITS**:

Rub 3 tablespoons (45g) cold **butter** together with a cup (140g) of **self-raising (self-rising) flour** and a good pinch of crushed **Maldon salt**, using both hands, until crumbly and sandlike. Add a quarter (60ml) cup **milk** mixed with a small squeeze of **fresh lemon juice** and stir in quickly with a fork just until incorporated. Turn onto the counter and knead gently a few times until the dough is slightly smoother. You don't want to overmix or overknead—you want them to be as light as your thighs. Press down gently into a rectangle about an inch thick. Use a wineglass to cut out three circles. Remove and flip each over and onto a baking sheet. Throw away the scraps.

Bake at 400°F (200°C) for about 15 minutes, until brown and puffy. Break off the top, jam in a good pat of butter, close, and let it melt right in there. What else can I say?

You'll definitely want a few cold beers with this—preferably **Coors Lite**, to bring home the whole look. Throw all the leg bones, wings, and smashed empty beer cans out your window.

QUARTER POUNDER WITH FRIES
(NOT MCDONALD'S)

See A Big Ol' Burger, page 134, and Frites, page 8. At least you won't feel sick afterward.

DINNER GUESTS

WHEN TO DELETE THEM FROM YOUR PHONE

When speaking to stupid people, intelligent guests must measure their words much more precisely, taking special care to avoid irony, which is usually lost on the simple-minded. If everyone at the table is stupid, it is most fortunate if they are all of phlegmatic temperament. If the reverse is true, it will be useful to play loud music during the meal.

—KARL FRIEDRICH VON RUMOHR, *The Essence of Cookery*, 1822

S: Hey, sweetie! I'm cooking for my birthday dinner on the twenty-fifth and would love to have you join . . .

Guest #1: I don't know (*yawns*), I may have an invite to an opening at the Serpentine that evening.

S: *May* have? Well, when will you know?

G1: Not till the day of.

S: But that's in three weeks.

G1: I know. It's very exclusive and there are limited invites. We're on a waitlist.

S: So . . . you're saying you want me to keep a free seat for you at my sit-down birthday dinner in case you don't get the invite?

G1: Yeah, that would be great. (*pause*) And can I bring my friend?

Because if he doesn't get the invite then we're both shit out of luck that night.

S: Who is he?

G1: I met him on Facebook. You won't know him, since you only have two people in your network.

S: So, save a place for you and your friend, whom I don't know, just in case.

G1: Uh, yes? Geez, what happened to your spontaneity? You're such a hater. It gets worse with age, huh?

Guest #2: . . . Oh, that is so sweet of you! I would love to! But I should let you know now that I've given up all meat, carbs, dairy, wheat, sugar, and alcohol. And I eat only wild-caught fish. Never farm raised.

S: Well, that's handy to know, thank you. We certainly don't want you spitting or hacking this time.

G2: I didn't know it was pork.

S: You were gagging as though you'd been poisoned.

G2: I *was* being poisoned.

S: It's not as if you were dying or something.

G2: You know I'm Jewish.

S: Well, yes, but since when have you become such a devoted Hasidic?

G2: You should respect our traditions.

S: Well, it's good you've forewarned me this time. So it'll be vegetable broth and water for you, then.

G2: Ha ha. Do you mind if I bring Jamie and his girlfriend? You'll love them—they're on the same detox as me.

S: Gee, this should be fun.

G2: By the way, who's coming? Last time, you had that awful man seated next to me—the one who went on and on about American capitalism versus British imperialism or some crap like that. For like forty-five minutes. His face never moved. Do you think he had Botox or something? He was creepy.

S: He was a hedge funder from L.A.

G2: I didn't know there were hedge funds in L.A. And another thing, can you keep the left-handed people at the left ends of the table? He kept banging into me with his elbow while he was eating and practically knocked my fork out of my hand. What a freak.

Guest #3: . . . is that on a Wednesday? Oh, darling, I have a yoga class till seven that evening that I absolutely cannot miss and my mani and pedi appointments are immediately before, so it'll be a bit hectic. Oh, and the nanny is on holiday for two weeks. A paid one, that is. The kids are terribly distraught and the new one is just, well, she's new . . . and pretty . . . I don't trust her. And Simon seems to have awful allergies this month—he's constantly sniffling. I'm not sure what that's all about. And have I told you our new driver has gotten at least thirteen parking tickets this month alone? He's incompetent. We're desperately searching for a new one. Such hassle, I can't believe how difficult it is. Oh! and Prince Charles! Have I told you? Prince Charles cannot be left alone anymore! The neighbors have a petition against his barking and say it's a disturbance of the peace. Can you believe it? They're so jealous. Would you mind terribly if I brought him along? He has abandonment issues. Poor little thing.

S: Okay. I'm going to go kill myself right now.

G3: So I have to get back to you on this one. You know I'll be moving mountains to make it possible. Lots of love. Bye-bye-bye-b-b-bye. Bye! Bye.

Guest #4: . . . are you cooking?

S: Of course!

G4: Because last time I threw up. I didn't want to say anything because you're really into your food and all, but I just had to let you know. It could have possibly been a food allergy, but honestly, darling, I don't think the scallops were that fresh.

S: But they were locally sourced.

G4: From the Thames?

S: Those scallops cost me a fortune and were hand-dived by a legendary one-armed fisherman in Cornwall.

G4: Uh, er . . . yeah, well, ask Sophie about it as well. She looked a little green when we got home too. Listen, darling, I have to run, Japan's on the other line, call me later.

S: Me call you . . . ?

Guest #5: (*voice mail*) Hey, it's Michael. Leave a message at the beep.

S: Hey, sweetie! I'm cooking for my birthday dinner on the twenty-fifth and would love to have you join. Let me know as soon as possible. Thanks!

(*to be continued . . .*)

Guest #6: What time?

S: Eight P.M. Sharp. You were almost two hours late last time.

G6: And your point? I recall not eating until, what was it? Eleven-fifteen, eleven-thirty?—"Suzanne's Estimated Time of Dining."

S: I was experimenting.

G6: That's great, but while you were doing your cheffy thing, the rest of us were famished and wasted.

S: I love it, you bring one bottle of wine and drink three. How does that work?

G6: I didn't know you were keeping count. I had to kill time because your guests were so unbelievably boring.

S: You seemed to get on quite well with Sophie. I recall walking in on the two of you in my bathroom. She was facing you . . . on her knees.

G6: What can I say? She was hungry.

S: Nice.

G6: (*snickers*) So maybe you'll finally crack open that expensive bottle of red I brought over two dinner parties ago? The one you stashed away? I was hoping to try it out. You should know it cost me sixty quid.

S: I drank it. Alone. It was delicious. Thank you.

Guest #7: Y'know, I must say I was really offended at your last dinner.

S: Wow, really? Why?

G7: I was really offended you didn't serve my cheese log. I offered to bring something.

S: And I said it wasn't necessary.

G7: And I did it anyway because that's how I am.

S: But that was your choice.

G7: I think you're really ungrateful. And snobby.

S: That's not very nice.

G7: What? Did I not bring the right "type" of cheese for your fancy schmancy pretentious dinner party?

S: You know, you're getting a little hostile there.

G7: I mean, share the bounty!

S: It was just too much food.

G7: If I'd put another label on the cheese, would you have served it then?

S: It was unnecessary. It didn't go . . . with . . .

G7: There! See! Ungrateful!

S: It just didn't work with the scallops.

G7: So now we're getting to the bottom of it. (*pause*) So, what did you do with it, then?

S: I threw out your fucking cheese log, okay?

G7: Whoa! Easy there, missy.

S: Your ugly stupid fucking fake cheese log. In the bin. To the vermin. Okay? Are you happy now?

G7: You know, you're really mean. Fuck your stupid dinner party. I hope you choke.

Guest #5 (. . . *continued*)

Twenty-one days have passed. It is the day of my birthday dinner, a few hours before . . .

S: (*voice mail*) "Hi, this is Suzanne. Please leave a message. Thanks."

G5: Hey! What's up? So what time should I be there tonight?

Why host a dinner party in a spirit of misguided enthusiasm? This collection of recipes is a celebration to dining alone: an ode to the Lucullus in you. Why would you ever want to waste expensive, well-sourced, and precious ingredients on a bunch of ingrates?

THREE-CHEESE RAVIOLI
WITH SHAVED WHITE TRUFFLES

Nurture the pastina[†] in yourself and make your own.

CHEESE FILLING

In a bowl, combine about 3 tablespoons each of grated **pecorino**, **parmigiano**, and **fresh sheep's milk ricotta cheese**. Add one small **egg**, beaten well, and a pinch of **Maldon salt.** Set aside.

PASTA

Mix 1¼ cups (165g) **flour** with a pinch of Maldon salt in a bowl. Beat two **eggs** well (use duck eggs for a richer dimension), make a well in the center, and add just enough of the beaten eggs to make a firm pasta dough. Now turn out onto your floured counter and knead well until the dough is as smooth as a baby's bum—about 10 minutes. Wrap the dough well in plastic wrap (so it doesn't get crusty) and let rest in the fridge for 30 minutes or so.

Cut the dough in half and flatten each piece into a rectangle. Using a rolling pin, roll out one piece on a lightly floured counter. You're aiming for a very very long rectangle. It'll be stiff, so roll up your sleeves and get in there. Use the length of your forearms for

---

[†] *Pastina*—a big old Italian lady with black whiskers sprouting from her chin. She rolls a mean pasta dough, though.

more power. Flip, dust the counter with flour, and keep rolling. Continue with this action. Roll it, baby. Roll it like there's no tomorrow. You want to be able to see straight through the dough. As soon as you think it's thin enough, roll again—so it's just at its tearing point. Repeat with the other half. Trim the edges.[‡]

Decide what shape and size ravioli you want (massive rounds, small squares, etc.?) and, according to size, place dollops of cheese filling in rows about two inches apart. Loosely place the other sheet of dough on top. Press the dough down firmly between the dollops of cheese and cut with a knife. Use your fingers to brush a little water around the edges of the bottom layer of the pasta if there's trouble making them stick. Make sure they're all securely sealed and have at least an inch trim around the edges.

Drop the ravioli in gently simmering salted water and cook for just a few minutes. When they're done, they'll all float to the top. Remove with a slotted spoon and place on a plate. Finish with melted **butter** (mix butter together with a little of the pasta water), shaved parmigiano, a pinch of Maldon salt and **cracked black pepper,** and **white Alba truffle shavings** (or if not in season, a nice drizzle of **white truffle oil** until they are).

White or red? Either works beautifully. Earthy truffles with an earthy **Barolo** from **Bruno Giacosa** or from **Giacomo Conterno**—an old one—twenty-five to thirty years. For a white burgundy, an '83 **Leflaive Bâtard Montrachet.**

[‡] Slice any scraps of dough into strips equal in length and about ⅕ inch wide. (You'll have enough for a portion.) Lay on a rack to dry. This is your *scialatielli,* or flat pasta. See Bonus Recipes (page 203) for a recipe to eat them with.

ROASTED LOBSTER

(a classic recipe inspired by Julia Child, who was inspired by Jasper White, who was inspired by Auguste Escoffier... who was inspired by Brillat-Savarin... who was inspired by Taillevant...)

The French like to gently stroke their lobsters to sleep just before the chef plunges a knife through the head and rips off the tail. Those guys are crazy. It's like a Tony Soprano setup: feed the guy some lasagna before he gets whacked. But in truth, it's actually the most humane method, as it causes an instantaneous death (unlike throwing the lobster in a pot of boiling water). Also, when they're calm before their final farewell, the meat remains tender.

Preheat the oven to 450°F (230°C). Bring a small pot of water to a simmer.

You'll need one **live fresh lobster**—about 1½ pounds. Place the lobster on a cutting board (don't forget to put wet paper towels or cloth underneath, to keep the board from slipping). Hold it gently by its tail and plunge a sharp heavy knife straight down to the board at the cross located at the very top of the tail (a few inches below the eyes) and split up through its head. This kills it instantly, but there may still be some twitching. It'll stop. Now split lengthwise down to the tail, keeping the meat in the shell. Twist off the tiny legs and discard. Twist off the claws and set aside. Remove and discard the black vein (intestinal channel) in the tail and the small gravel sack (the stomach). Some people love the green liver (tomalley) mixed with butter and served with the lobster meat. They say it's a delicacy. I think it's disgusting. But perhaps I'll acquire a taste for it one day.

So, where were we? Okay, poach the claws for 2 to 3 minutes, cool, crack open the shells, and remove the meat. Set aside.

In a little hot **olive oil**, sear the lobster tail halves shell side down in an ovenproof skillet. They'll become red quickly—turn them over and sear on the other side. Place the skillet in the hot oven for several minutes more, but do not overcook. Slightly undercook, if anything—they'll continue to cook while they rest, as you know. Place the lobster tail halves on your dinner plate.

Sweat a finely chopped **shallot** (a small teaspoonful) gently in olive oil. Deglaze with a little **cognac** off the heat. Bring the pan back to the burner—carefully—and burn off the alcohol. I'm not a big flambé person, particularly after watching Tony Soprano's lover light herself on fire while preparing an omelet. She was pretty scary-looking afterward—all bandaged up and in the hospital. Yikes.

Add about half a cup of **white wine** and the **claw meat**. Reduce the liquid till it thickens to a mere few tablespoons. Now add the **butter**—a small spoonful at a time (two to four spoonfuls will be enough—your call), gently shaking the pan back and forth until the sauce begins to emulsify. Season with a bit of **sea salt** and ground **white pepper**. Remove from heat and stir in some freshly chopped **chives** and **tarragon**. Spoon over your little baby lobster.

Lobster aches for a concentrated white with good acidity. A white Burgundy, such as a **Puligny** or **Chassagne Montrachet**, matches the luxuriousness of the lobster. But why limit oneself? **Chenin Blanc** from the Loire is a perfect companion as well.

PAN-SEARED WAGYU STEAK

*Preferably an A5 Japanese grade. I need to be assured that my
Wagyu cow had been pampered with daily spa treatments—
manicures, pedicures, and full-body massages (with release).*

Heat a heavy frying pan, without oil, till smoking. Sprinkle a filet of
Wagyu strip steak with **Maldon salt** and **crushed black pepper**
on each side. Sear the narrow sides first for about 20 to 30 seconds
each and then the flat sides—about 1 to 2 minutes each side. Don't
fiddle—you want a gorgeous brown crust to form (it will be quick).
If you'd like, add a tablespoon of butter, tilt the pan to one side till
the butter foams, add a small branch of rosemary to infuse it for a
minute, and spoon it over the top. Take out the steak and let it rest
for a minute. No knife will be necessary because it really does melt
in your mouth.

How about a glass of **Pétrus**—a toast to Merlot, and those two
clowns in *Sideways*.

SEA URCHIN RISOTTO

Sea urchins are seasonal and somewhat difficult to find—but you must. I was lucky enough to find sea urchins from Orkney, sold by Miguel Antunes at the Borough Market stand in London called Orkney Rose. The shell is delicate and easy to work with. You'll just have to be a little brave and get in there. I think it's important to try it as seviche first before you begin to play around, if you haven't already had them at Nobu.

Place a cloth around the **sea urchin** and, using kitchen scissors, push one blade into the tip of the "mouth"—which is the tiny white dot and soft part in the center. It looks like a little flower bud, if you inspect it closely. Cut out a disk about 2 to 3 inches (as you would a coconut). It will come out really easily. You'll see lots of seawater— gently pour it out and reserve. At the bottom, you'll see the coral— about four to five orange clusters. Carefully spoon them out and set aside. Discard everything else.

Drizzle one or two of the clusters with a little **yuzu lime juice** (or fresh squeezed lime and lemon), a tiny dash of **olive oil**, if desired, and a sprinkling of **fleur de sel** and let sit for a few minutes, then eat.

Weird but extraordinary, eh? Okay, now try this:

In a medium pan, sauté two cleaned and sliced **squid** in a little hot olive oil, just until opaque. Set aside and keep warm. Throw in a few handfuls of cleaned and tightly shut **mussels**, pour in a cup of the **white wine** you are drinking (or water), cover with a lid, and cook till the mussels open—a few minutes. Remove the mussels and reserve the liquid.

In same pan, sweat a tablespoon of minced **shallots** and one or two minced **garlic cloves** until soft but not brown. Add half a cup **Carnaroli rice** and cook over low heat until translucent—a few minutes. Deglaze with the reserved liquid from the mussels and let it reduce until almost absorbed. Stir in about half a cup hot **fish stock** and let the rice absorb it, cooking slowly before adding another half a cup. Stir in a pinch of **saffron threads**. Add the reserved seawater (strain if necessary). By this point, your risotto should have a little bite to it and should be swollen and lovely. If not, add a little more fish stock and let it be absorbed a bit longer.

Remove the mussels from the shells and add to the risotto along with the squid, 1 or 2 tablespoons of **Échiré butter**, and a squeeze of **lemon**. Cover and let sit for a few minutes. Season with fleur de sel, **white pepper**, and chopped **fresh flat-leaf parsley**. Ladle onto a plate. Top with the remaining sea urchin coral and stir in. This truly adds a whole other dimension—the risotto will be creamy and decadent and taste like the ocean. It's quite extraordinary.

You can also stir the coral at the very end into scrambled eggs; into spaghetti mixed with butter, a squeeze of lemon, and chopped flat-leaf parsley; or into a beurre blanc sauce and over onto a mild white fish, such as sea bass or flounder; or use in foams and sauces for the cheffy thing. Although I still just like it *au naturel.*

The creamy texture and briny flavor of the sea urchin beckon whites with a crisp freshness and a whiff of sea air. A **Ligurian Pigato** and **Cinque Terre** would be lovely.

CROQUE MONSIEUR WITH
SMOKED SALMON AND CAVIAR

I've been making this Eric Ripert recipe for the past ten years. And recently Amanda Hesser dug it up for her Recipe Redux in the New York Times, *refining every last detail. It's a classic for me—and the perfect midnight sandwich snack.*

Cut two very thin slices of **brioche**. Cover one piece with very thin slices of **Gruyère cheese** and the other with a few slices of **Scottish smoked salmon**. Sprinkle the salmon with finely grated **lemon zest** and minced **chives**. Then spread some **osetra caviar** over the salmon. Close it up.

Spread a little softened **Échiré butter** on both sides of the sandwich. Heat a frying pan and add the sandwich, cheese side down. Cook for a few minutes till brown, flip, and brown the other side for a minute, till golden.

Use any leftover caviar within one week, or be sensible, and repeat this for breakfast.

And for that nightcap with your snack, a **Gewürztraminer**. First pronounce it. Go on. "Guh-vehrtz-tra-meena," but with a heavy German accent (Alsatian, really, but that's trickier). And to look the part of a German, you'll need the skill of a ventriloquist, or a ton of Botox (keep mouth and face immobile and expressionless). Now say **Clos Windsbuhl** from **Zind Humbrecht.** Or the **Domaine Trimbach, Cuvée des Seigneurs de Ribeaupierre**. Go on. You'll be a hit in your wine shop.

ESCALOPE OF FOIE GRAS WITH WILD MUSHROOMS AND AGED BALSAMIC

To enjoy in the comfort and privacy of your own home. PETA's not invited.

Sauté a good handful of cleaned and sliced **wild mushrooms**—chanterelles, blue foot, and other seasonal varieties—over a high flame in a few drops of **olive oil**. Pour off any liquid generated before adding a little **butter**, a finely chopped **garlic clove**, and some chopped **fresh flat-leaf parsley.** Season well. Remove and keep warm.

Make sure any fat and connective tissue or veins have been removed from your nice 1-inch escalope of room temperature **duck foie gras**. (Have your butcher be a chum and sell you a slice. If he sucks you into buying the whole thing, see page 198 for more recipes.) **Salt** and **pepper** each side and coat very lightly in **flour**. Wipe out the mushroom pan and heat over a very high flame. The pan needs to be just smoking—but do not overheat, you don't want the foie gras to melt. Place the foie gras in the pan—it should sizzle loudly. Sear 1 to 1½ minutes on each side. Drain on paper towels. Spoon the mushrooms onto the plate and top with the foie gras and a drizzle of the best **aged balsamic vinegar** you can find.

Serve with some freshly toasted **peasant bread** and a chilled glass of something spectacular. A '67 **Château d'Yquem** Sauternes is stunning, yet safe, for the pretentious lot, but why not a **Tokaji Aszu** from Hungary or a **Vin Santo** from Tuscany? The older the better, to balance the balsamic notes and earthiness of the mushrooms.

"YOU WANNA KNOW HOW I GOT THESE SCARS?"

HOW TO LOOK (AND COOK) LIKE A BADASS

Frailty, thy name is woman!

—SHAKESPEARE, *Hamlet*

Last year, I was asked to cook in a live demonstration called "Celebrity Chefs in London" at Olympia Exhibition Hall for a Christmas fair. The lineup of chefs was impressive, and I was honored to be part of it. Now don't get me wrong, I certainly have no delusions about where I am in the pecking order—whether I'm regarded as a chef, a cook, a washed-up-has-been-who's-never-been, who cares? I think the woman in charge was just desperate to fill the slot.

Before my debut, one of the big chefs stopped me. "Why are you here?" he asked. "You're not a chef. You don't look like a chef." And just to hammer it in he said, "You'd never last a day in my kitchen."

Interesting. I politely refrained from commenting on his Primark shoes and sad sack hairdo.

Funny thing is, I had worked in his kitchen. And he was right. I didn't last a day. I lasted half a day—in a *stage* that ended quickly.

The truth was, I was bored. Bored *at* the sight of his brigade of all-male chefs, bored of his menu, but mostly, bored of him. He spent far *far* too much time talking to me—and not about cooking either, if you know what I'm saying . . .

"So how many women do you have in your kitchen these days?" I asked. "I was just wondering how long you were planning on keeping women out of your kitchen so you can perpetuate your idea of what a stereotypical female chef should look like. Whatever that is." I again politely refrained from commenting on his tired eighties French cuisine or the chip on his shoulder for having never received a second Michelin star.

It was certainly interesting to be standing across from this revered chef and cooking at the same event. And although I would never have this dinosaur's experience or credentials, it was obvious that his sole mission now was to be out of the kitchen and into a nice little Faustian bargain with television fame and fortune. The problem was he had the appeal of Horace Fungusdick and the charm of Michel Merde.

When I was sixteen, I decided I wanted to pursue cooking as a formal career. I had spent two summers working in a local restaurant in New York (I lied about my age so I could work), going from dishwasher to prep cook, garde manger to chef de partie. I had also been teaching myself how to cook and practicing on my family and our friends every weekend since about the age of seven.

The Culinary Institute of America in Hyde Park, New York, was my next step and only consideration. When my dad drove me up for the interview, I didn't see one woman on campus. Or a woman who may have resembled a woman. The majority of students were what appeared to be ex-convicts on Harley-Davidsons, complete with shaved heads, burly goatees, and bad boy biker tattoos (although some tattoos read "Mom" across a beautiful heart, which I thought was really sweet; Dad, however, did not). This was definitely not an option.

Still, life went on, and many years later and not quite sure where it would lead, I finally satisfied my recurring itch to prepare exquisite food—only now with proper training (forget New York—why not Paris?). I begged, barged, and wheedled my way into any kitchen that would have me and worked until I had had enough. Enough of the madness. It certainly created some interesting stories.

A few years ago I did a *stage* in another Michelin-starred restaurant. The prep was standard (endless), but the best bit was stepping back and simply observing. The minute that first order came in, the chef—very slight in build and ordinarily somewhat shy—would transform into a sadistic crackpot. Once the apron went on, he became Mr. Hyde—with Tourette's. It was spellbinding. He tormented, humiliated, yelled, screamed, and shouted every expletive imaginable at every member of his staff—at every line cook, every server, every busboy—for five hours, at bloodcurdling volume: *"Where are my foie gras beignets, you fucking cunt, you fucking stupid piece of shit, you fucking useless scum—how long? Is that thirteen seconds or fourteen, you fucking twat, you fucking . . ."* and on and on and on and on.

Yet after the last order went out, he calmly removed his apron and wriggled out of his kitchen as a calm and cool Dr. Jekyll—in a pair of tight Seven jeans. When he offered me the job, I looked around at yet another all-male chef brigade—all of whom must have had an IQ of 45 (why else would they stay—he's not *that* talented), subjecting themselves to the daily torture of debasement in hell. It was so utterly tragic, it was comical. I had to squelch my laugh. This place was a madhouse. I now understood why open kitchens were becoming so popular.

A few months later, I started in the pastry section of yet another newly Michelin-starred restaurant. When I arrived at 7:30 A.M., I found myself working alongside two young men. Shocker. I did see one woman in the garde manger section. With her skeletal frame, she looked like a prisoner of war in a chef's jacket and checkered pants. I suspected that if she ever collapsed, the others would walk right over her body, smirking. Or better, an ambitious sycophant would discreetly carry her away, chop off her leg, french the bone, and braise it—then show off his miraculous way with a lamb-type shank to the head chef.

So the three of us worked together in a six-by-six-foot space for eighteen hours straight, under fluorescent lights and with zero break. You were a wimp if you took one. It's amazing how slave labor still prevails in so many cosmopolitan cities. I would always volunteer to temper the chocolate, because the workspace was set outside. I had to work fast because it was freezing, but at least I could combat the economy-class syndrome overtaking my body.

Back in my section, one pastry chef was also about to kick it. His face was colorless and his BO was abominable. Aside from never seeing the light of day and never showering, he was a frenetic mess. He later revealed that he had just spent a year in the kitchen I had just come from and said he was still "recovering" from it but "needed to be there because it was good training."

"Why are *you* here?" he asked. "You don't look like a chef." And in a paranoid panic, he began ordering me around in his best attempt at an alpha male braggadocio chef stereotype. It never ends.

I guess I'd have to look like I'm about to die to be taken seriously as a chef. Otherwise, I'm only a mere "cook"—or worse, a spy, which I've also been called. The truth is, even today, it's still pretty rare to find a woman in any professional kitchen—whatever she may look like.

These recipes are a tribute to the great female chefs who have all hung in there and made a name for themselves. Hats off to you, ladies.

CALAMAR RELLENO CON SETAS Y VEGETALES

(Mushroom- and Vegetable-Stuffed Squid)

This tasty and hearty Catalan recipe was generously given to me by Spain's first three-starred Michelin chef, Carme Ruscalleda. She is only the second woman in the world to receive three stars. She's still in the kitchen cooking, at her restaurant, Sant Pau (or checking in on her Japanese location), and couldn't be kinder.

line-caught squid—one, approximately half a pound (250g)
olive oil
sea salt and **white pepper**
leek—a quarter, julienned
garlic and **flat-leaf parsley**—a small amount of each, finely chopped
tiny zucchini squash—julienned
chanterelle mushrooms—a very large handful
porcini mushrooms—another large handful
tomato—one, ripe, medium, seeded, and very finely chopped
dry sherry—a splash

First clean the squid, making sure the skin comes off and it doesn't get stained with ink from the ink sac. Dry very well, inside and out. Slice off the tentacles. Next, use olive oil to coat all sides of the body and tentacles, then sprinkle with sea salt and sear on a very hot griddle (or in nonstick frying pan) until deep golden brown. This should take no more than 3 minutes. Set aside.

In the same frying pan, sauté each of the following ingredients separately with sea salt and white pepper to taste: the leek (along with the garlic and parsley), the zucchini, and finally the chanterelle and porcini mushrooms.

Mix all the sautéed ingredients together and stuff the squid—it must be well packed. Close each end with a toothpick, cut the squid in half in order to speed up the final cooking process, and close the cut ends with toothpicks as well.

Sauté the tomato in a little olive oil for 5 minutes—or until quite soft. Season. In a small individual casserole dish, spread out the tomato and place the squid, along with the tentacles, on top of the tomato, then drizzle with a little olive oil and a small splash of sherry. Bake at 375°F (190°C) for 4 to 5 minutes until piping hot and bubbling.

Sip with a glass of **Manzanilla sherry**, which has a briny intensity and is great with seafood. Try a **Papirusa** bottling from Lustau.

CLIPS DE COGOLLOS CON MANGO
(Lettuce Heart Clips with Mango)

I love the translated names of recipes. Some sound ludicrously unappealing. But in this case, Elena Arzak has yet again created something truly out of this world here, full of subtle surprises that linger with decadence and kick. And the biggest catch: no equipment—which would seem virtually impossible given her molecular gastronomic style of cooking. (I cringed as I discussed the premise of this book with her very protective and very thorough assistant, Monica—being careful not to disrespect the integrity of her style.) With three Michelin stars at the famous Restaurante Arzak in San Sebastián, she still cooks every day alongside her dad, Juan Mari, known as the father of modern Basque cuisine (and Ferran's mentor).

SLICES OF MANGO
> **half a mango**
> **sugar**

Peel and very thinly slice the mango, keeping the slices as long and wide as possible. (You'll be stuffing and rolling them up later on.) Sprinkle both sides very lightly with sugar and place in a hot frying pan to caramelize. Test one before proceeding with the rest, so you get the gist of it and can adjust the heat accordingly. After a minute or two, it'll start to become golden around the edges. Flip over and repeat. Lift off carefully with a spatula and set aside on parchment, so that they don't stick.

FOIE GRAS FILLING

foie gras—one fresh thick slice (about 50g)

crema de queso ("cream of cheese"—I substituted mascarpone)—1½ tablespoons

extra virgin olive oil

ground ginger

salt and **black pepper**

Dice and sauté the foie gras. Let rest for 5 minutes and mince together with the cheese and a very tiny drizzle of olive oil. Season with a pinch each of ground ginger, salt, and black pepper. Set aside.

LETTUCE HEART

lettuce heart—one, such as the heart of iceberg or baby Gem Romaine.

0,4 percent extra virgin olive oil—0,4 percent being the degree of acidity. The lower, the more superior. (You never want it to be above 1 percent.)

salt and **pepper**

Finely slice the lettuce heart lengthways and lightly drizzle with olive oil to keep it from turning brown. Season with salt and pepper and set aside.

ripe tomato—one

black truffle juice—a teaspoon

sherry vinegar—a teaspoon

powdered caramel—a tablespoon. To make it: over medium heat, caramelize 3 tablespoons **sugar** in a stainless steel pan until golden. Will be quick because there's such a small amount, so pay attention! Quickly turn onto greased parchment paper. Let cool, then crush in mortar and pestle until powdered.

0,4 percent extra virgin olive oil

ground ginger

sea salt

Scoop out the pulp and seeds of the tomato and press through a sieve. Reserve the seeds. Set the tomato aside. Then whisk together with all the other ingredients and set aside. (You may want to double or triple this recipe, because it is stunning.) Use the tomato to make tomato bread.[†]

PRESENTATION

Place a small spoonful of the foie filling in the center of a mango slice. Pull the mango slice over the filling, tuck the ends in, and roll up. Ideally, you want it to look like a little package, but it'll

---

[†] Tomato bread is a traditional starter you see in Catalan cooking and at many tapas bars. Take the tomato and rub it well against toasted ciabatta until the tomato is demolished. It'll make the bread slightly wet and tomatoey. You can now drizzle it with extra virgin olive oil or use for dunking with an olive oil/garlic-based dish (such as Basquian Lemon Shrimp on page 113).

depend on the size of your mango slices. Either way, it'll still taste amazing.

Place a few mango parcels in a line across a plate (three is always a good number) with a little shredded lettuce beside each. Drizzle the lettuce heart with the tomato seed vinaigrette. Just a fun little snack. Even better with a small glass of **Muscat de Beaumes**, as Colum suggests. He also reiterates that for those with their head up their butt about sweet wines—first, pull it out. Because this wine is fortified, it will be rich and not too sweet with tropical notes that work beautifully.

RISTRETTO DI PISELLI CON GNOCCHETTI DI PANE ALL'UVA E FRESCO DI CAPRA

(Cream of Peas, Raisin Bread Gnocchetti, and Fresh Goat Cheese)

Luisa Marelli Valazza's interpretation of a classic Italian peasant soup at her three-Michelin-starred restaurant, Al Sorriso in Piedmont, is hands-down stunning. It's a hearty and rustic showstopper: thick and creamy fresh pea soup with tiny gnocchetti made from raisin pumpernickel bread. Great on a cold and rainy spring evening (fresh pea season). Luisa said it was three simple steps, but it's a little more than that...

SOUP

scallion—half, minced

butter—a tablespoon

potato—one small, unpeeled, scrubbed, and cut into small dice

peas—fresh, about two handfuls

chicken stock—about 2 cups

GNOCCHETTI

leek heart—half, finely chopped

butter

fresh raisin pumpernickel (black) bread—a slice, crust removed, and minced

nutmeg—freshly grated

salt and **black pepper**

egg—one, small and beaten well

GARNISH

whole peas—a few

tomato—a tablespoon, brunoised

goat cheese—a quenelle—or a spoonful of a soft, creamy young
one

extra virgin olive oil—drizzle

chervil—a little, freshly chopped

Brown the scallion in the butter. Add the potatoes and sauté until
they are light golden in color. Add the peas (save a few for garnish),
then about a cup of the stock, and let it all simmer for about 15 minutes, until soft. Add more stock if necessary. It should be liquidy.

Meanwhile, for the gnocchetti, sweat the leek in butter. Stir in
the bread and season with freshly grated nutmeg, salt, and pepper.
Place the mixture in a small bowl and mix in just enough beaten
egg to make it slightly wet. Scoop out small quarter size balls, place
in the palm of your hand, and gently squeeze down till compressed
to mold into *gnocchetti* (baby gnocchi).

Make sure the peas and potatoes are soft and pour the mixture
through a sieve, pressing the vegetables through with a rubber spatula. The pressing should yield about a cup or a cup and a half. Add a
little more stock if the soup is too thick. Strain again if necessary
and pour into a small saucepan. Drop in several gnocchetti, cover,
and heat through at low heat for a few minutes until piping hot.

Pour carefully into a heated soup bowl, to keep those little babies intact. Garnish with the fresh peas, tomato, goat cheese, a drizzle of an excellent extra virgin olive oil, and chopped chervil.

Beautiful with the wonderfully crafted **Vieris Isonzo Sauvignon** from Gianfranco Gallo's Vie di Romans property.

SOFT-SHELL CRABS WITH LIMA BEAN SALAD, GRILLED BACON, AND CORNBREAD

*It's August, and Suzanne Goin is in Los Angeles running her three restaurants, **Lucques**, AOC, and **The Hungry Cat**, while pregnant and looking after her baby twins. To ask her to create a new recipe for me would be a little selfish, so we decided I'd choose a dish from* Sunday Suppers at Lucques. *Her soft-shell crabs are a delectable summer treat, and perfect for just one. They're super-easy to prepare for yourself—and with this recipe you can take advantage of the bountiful surplus of beans readily available at this time. It's so much quicker to shell a few handfuls for yourself than to devote a day to shelling pound after pound for a family.*

LIMA BEAN SALAD

Heat a small saucepan and swirl in a tablespoon of **olive oil**. Add a tablespoon of finely diced **onion**, a small minced **garlic clove**, and a pinch of **fresh thyme leaves**, and sweat for a few minutes. Add half a cup to three-quarters cup freshly shelled **lima beans** and stir to coat the beans with the onion and oil. Season with **salt** and **pepper**, then add enough water to cover the beans by a few inches. Simmer five to seven minutes, until the beans are just tender. Cool before tossing into a vinaigrette of a little minced **shallot**, a squeeze of

lemon juice, a little olive oil, chopped **opal basil** and **fresh flat-leaf parsley**, and seasoned with salt and pepper.

CORNBREAD

Heat a small individual cast-iron skillet and carefully melt 2 tablespoons butter, swirling until just browned. Remove from heat.

Combine half a cup (100g) **cornmeal**, half a cup (70g) **flour**, one tablespoon **sugar**, ¾ teaspoon **baking powder**, a tiny pinch of **baking soda**, and a good pinch of **kosher salt**. Make a well in center and add one small **egg**, half a cup plus two tablespoons **buttermilk** (milk plus a tablespoon of fresh squeezed lemon juice to equal half a cup), and a tablespoon **honey**, and very lightly mix—do not overwork the batter. Fold in the brown butter.

Add a tablespoon of butter again to the cast-iron pan and melt till bubbly. Remove from the heat, pour in the batter, and bake at 400°F (200°C) for 15 to 20 minutes, until golden brown and set.

SOFT-SHELL CRABS

Using scissors, clean two or three jumbo **soft-shell crabs** (Maryland blue, from the Chesapeake Bay) to remove the gills, the pouch, and then the eyes. Dredge the crabs in **Wondra flour** (the best choice for a delicate and crisp crust), and season them with pepper. Heat a frying pan, add ¼-inch olive oil, and place in the crabs upside down. Sauté about five minutes without moving the crabs, until that side is crisp. Flip and cook a few minutes. Peek under the shell to check that the flesh is opaque. Remove.

Meanwhile, grill a few thick slabs of **applewood smoked bacon** till crisp, and drain on a paper towel. Slice the cornbread into a few half-inch-thick slices and butter them lightly. Grill on both sides till brown.

ASSEMBLY

Mix a few spoonfuls of **crème fraîche** with a little **whole grain mustard** and set aside. Place the grilled cornbread on a plate. Scatter over some fresh **arugula**, top with the grilled bacon, spoon on the lima bean salad, and place the crabs on top. Dollop on the mustard crème fraîche.

The sweetness of the crab and the lima beans would take well to a chenin blanc—based wine, and the best are from the Loire. Try a **Savennières**, a good and dry **Vouvray**, or a **Montiouis**, which are your best options.

GRILLED PEACHES WITH AMARETTO

You can never really get enough of The River Cafe in London. And to actually see either Ruth Rogers or Rose Gray cooking behind that long counter each and every time I dine there is undeniably impressive. For this reason (and not to mention some of the best food in London), they are legendary. I won't mention how many great chefs' careers have been launched there as well. Here's a little bone they threw me! Simplicity at its best.

Preheat the oven to 375°F (190°C).

Take a **peach**, cut it in half, and remove the stone. Carefully place the peach halves, cut side down, and cook on a skillet grill until each half has become slightly charred.

Slice a **vanilla pod** lengthwise and scrape the beans out and into a mortar and pestle. Add two tablespoons **sugar** and pound with the pestle until broken up and combined.

Place the peach halves faceup in a shallow ovenproof baking dish. Scatter the vanilla sugar over them and pour in a dash of **Amaretto**. Place in the oven and bake for ten minutes, or until the peaches are soft. Pour over another dash of Amaretto and serve hot or cold with a dollop of **crème fraîche**.

Continue sipping with a little Amaretto if you'd like, or have with a French **Sauternes** or **Barsac**—a classic pairing with peaches.

ON GRAZING

All sorrows are less with bread.

—MIGUEL DE CERVANTES, *Don Quixote*

It was seven o'clock in the morning when the phone rang. It was my boyfriend's mother, which was unusual. I thought about bolting across my studio apartment to answer it, but as I listened to her voice on my answering machine, I knew something was wrong. If I had to deal with something big that day, I needed to prepare for it. I needed my strength. I went back to sleep.

Three days later, I walked into his family's church, haunted. My eyes were practically swollen shut, and I couldn't focus much on anything. Drifting through a low-grade murmur, I made my way over to his coffin. Seeing him made up like a drag queen was shocking. Why do they do that? I decided then that I definitely would like to be burned. I knelt in front of him and held his cold, rocklike hand. I leaned in and kissed his lips. I placed my favorite picture of the two of us inside his suit pocket. I'm not sure why I brought that picture with me in the first place. I sat with him for a while before someone took me away.

Everyone deals with tragedy differently. I decided to return to my waitressing job on 15th and 5th in Manhattan, but after I spent several continuous days of stuttering to customers, tears incessantly streaming down my face, they suggested that it might be wise to take some time off.

I hadn't really eaten much since my last meal of toast and Bustelo coffee the morning of that phone call. I had been subsisting mostly on a diet of cigarettes, coffee, and any sedative I could finagle without resorting to a prescription. I was twenty-four and couldn't afford health insurance. I smoked all the time. From the second I woke up, all during the day, and in bed—before dozing off at night. Food never entered my mind.

After a good month of complete solitude, I slowly began to integrate into the world. I started getting compliments from all the girls I hated. "You look great." "Wow, you've never looked better." Which was disturbing because my clothes were hanging off me, I had a hacking cough from Marlboro Red–induced emphysema, and I hadn't slept in weeks. I was in bad shape, and knew I needed to begin again somewhere. I stepped over the pile of Fassbinder and Bergman films in my den of mourning hell and chain-smoked my way to the Farmers Market in Union Square, hacking along the way.

I'd like to wax lyrical over what some would describe as pure sensory overload—the vibrancy of ebullient colors, smells, and sounds, beginning with the array of summer fruits in all their blazing glory, crimson red to deep purple berries bursting next to heaping cartons of fat and juicy blueberries and just-plucked cherries, fuzzy white peaches and crates of glistening plums, piles and piles of tomatoes, from bright orange and golden yellow teardrops to monstrously bulbous Jersey beefsteaks, and dozens of lush and fragrant green herbs, serene beneath the sunny beaming faces of four-foot-tall sunflowers—but all I remember was the smell of steaming piss emanating from Union Square station below on a swelteringly brutal August day.

I walked over to the pretzel lady. She looked at me slightly aghast. I mean, I knew I looked bad, but geez. She gave me a bag of broken pretzels. Gratis. "You could use them," she said. I nibbled on a few and walked over to the cheese man. I handed him a ten-dollar bill for a small tub of goat cheese drizzled with olive oil and topped with pink and black peppercorns. Along with my change, he threw in a hunk of something else.

"It's my homemade sheep's—I think you'll like it," he winked. "Hey, darlin' . . . !" he gestured to the woman a few stalls over. "That's my daughter," he said, and smiled proudly as she handed him a baguette. He threw that into my bag too. I backed away and continued over to a fruit and vegetable vendor, where I paid for a pint of heirloom tomatoes and two peaches but also walked away with a handful of opal basil, a few sprigs of mint, and a perfectly contorted yellow summer squash. They just kept chucking things into my bag.

It suddenly occurred to me that they had mistaken me for a homeless or other unfortunate person. I decided to milk it for all it was worth. As I dragged my feet wearily over to the fish guy, he wrapped a fillet of deep reddish-orange king salmon at record speed and handed it to me. As I looked up at him and counted each dollar bill with the most woeful eyes I could muster, he stared at me confused, and grabbed his money. I really thought they had all pitied me, but realized it was the end of the day and they just needed to get rid of the stuff.

I won't indulge a foodie sentimentality that I was resurrected by the Farmers Market, because I wasn't, but I will admit that when I came upon this particular fork in the road, it was the wiser choice.

My first real meal consisted of:

- Sliced king salmon sashimi from the (stingy) fish guy, a sprinkle of salt, and a squeeze of lemon. Not a lot of love here, but a good start. Actually, it was succulent.

- A few slices of the daughter's freshly made baguette, toasted, with a drizzle of olive oil and hastily chopped heirlooms with a smashed garlic clove, a scattering of torn opal basil and fresh mint, sea salt, and cracked pepper spooned on top. Perfect.

- A few slices of her dad's sheep's milk cheese with a few slices of a juicy, fuzzy peach, a drizzle of honey, and one crackling of black pepper. Bliss.

- Biscotti ends, donated by the generous pastry chef at my restaurant. Jaw-breakingly stale without coffee, but comfortingly familiar.

Grazing like a cow all day long is quite restorative. The little meals. *La tapa. Mezze. Dim sum. Stuzzichini.* The Spanish king Alfonso the Tenth invented the word "tapas" because he had to take small bites of food due to illness. But given the era it was probably syphilis or something, so I have little sympathy. Anyway, my market became kind of a playground, and each season shaped my inspiration. I was really keen on seeing how little I had to do in preparing these "meals." The more seasonal, the fresher, the less I'd fiddle. It's a stupid waste of time messing with perfection. And this, well, yes, may just have resurrected me.

There's not much to any of these recipes, as you'll see, only the exceptional ingredients—which means no Frankenstein fish or genetically modified produce.

As for wine pairings in this chapter, Colum has a few thoughts:

To properly pair any wine with a dish, never ignore the spirit of the dish, and the spirit of these dishes is freshness. Light, bright whites and fragrant rosés are the way to go here. These dishes exalt the freshness of their ingredients and sing with vibrant energy. So when reaching for my wine rack, I'm not looking for anything redder than a rosé. Save your fancy reds for the other chapters.

Avoid whites that have sacrificed their freshness for the complexity of French oak. Even the oft-maligned Pinot Grigio will work here. The best of the Pinot Grigios are crafted by artisan vintners working in smaller vineyards—enabling them to administer greater attention to their vines, thereby harvesting better quality fruit. They are also producers who are more intent on representing their territory and tradition than getting a ninety-plus score from the latest and most fashionable wine critic. Theirs are honest, real wines.

I'm convinced that the reason that more people don't drink whites and rosés is that most wines available to them are produced by large corporations (no matter how they try to convince you otherwise) to whom quantity, profit, and advertising always come before quality. Speak with a knowledgeable wine clerk and ask about crisp, fresh wines that haven't seen oak treatment.

For whites, look for muscadet, chenin blanc, and sauvignon blanc–based wines from the Loire Valley; Alsatian, Austrian, and German Rieslings; the bright, mineral-laced whites from the Alto Adige or Friuli; and the crisp, lightly herbal wines of Campania. For rosés, I often feel the most interesting ones come from the warmer climates—like Puglia, Sicily, the valley floor in the Alto Adige, Tavel in the southern Rhône Valley, and Spain. There are many more of both.

Again, think of the spirit, weight, and key flavors of the dish and try to find a wine that has similar characteristics. For example, Sea Scallops with Seaweed Butter: sweetness (scallops), brininess (nori), acidity (lemon), and richness (butter). Two possibilities would be Manzanilla sherry or Vermentino from Liguria. They are whites grown in proximity to the sea and have sweetness, brininess, acidity, and richness. Perfect! Pissaladière: sweetness (onions and garlic), more brininess (anchovies and olives), richness (anchovy again), and aromatics (thyme and olives). A bracing Tavel with its acidity, perfume, and richer fruit flavors is perfect.

Once you've learned to appreciate these types of wine, you can then decide whether to turn your friends on to them or keep the pleasure to yourself!

WILD SEA BREAM SEVICHE

Whichever fish you choose for your seviche, it must be the absolute freshest it can be—practically alive—whether you fillet it yourself or not. I've chosen sea bream here because it's ample for a single portion and easy for a fishmonger to fillet it for you right there on the spot—if you won't yourself. Any other small whole white fish will be lovely as well. Experiment.

Slice the fillet[†] along the grain in strips (or small cubes) and place in a bowl. Squeeze the juice from a fresh **lime** until covered to "cook" it. Then combine freshly squeezed **lemon** and **orange juice** and a pinch each of **sugar** and **sea salt** and pour on top. Add in paper-thin sliced **fennel**, a few of its fuzzy **fennel tops** (pluck them off), coarsely chopped **cilantro** and **basil**, and a tiny minced **red chile**. Place in the fridge for 30 minutes to marinate. Serve alongside mixed greens. Perfect.

[†] Pan-sear the fillet for a few seconds on each side if you're having any reservations regarding the freshness of the fish. This will no longer be a true seviche but a recipe for . . . pan-seared fish. Tra la la.

SEA SCALLOPS WITH SEAWEED BUTTER

In Botticelli's Birth of Venus, *the Roman goddess of love and beauty emerges from the water on a giant gilded scallop shell. You don't have to eat this naked by the sea, although it would probably taste even better if you did. (Although while I was dining naked at Joël Robuchon's L'Atelier, in Paris—where the recipe has been adapted from—I must say, I enjoyed it very much.)*

Brush a couple of **hand-dived sea scallops**[†] all over with soft unsalted **butter**, place one in each shell (if available), and refrigerate until the butter is firm, 10 to 15 minutes. Preheat the broiler. Sprinkle the scallops with a pinch of finely chopped **nori**. Dot with a little more butter. Place the scallops in their shells (if using) or in a small baking dish and broil nori side up till barely cooked through—2 or 3 minutes. They'll rest for another minute, meaning they'll still be cooking as you bring them from oven to plate. They must be slightly translucent inside—otherwise they're already tough and will taste

---

[†] If you can get them live and in their shells, excellent. *To open scallops:* hold a scallop in your hand with the rounded side down. Insert the tip of a small knife close to the hinge and twist gently to sever the muscle and separate the shell. Work the knife in further if necessary and slide around the shell. Open. Gently ease out the scallop with a small spoon. Pull away the dark organs, the fringelike membrane, and the orange coral and discard. Rinse under cold water. Clean the shell in scalding hot water and set aside to dry.

like they've been frozen. And then what's the point? I can get a slice of rubber from my sneakers.

Transfer the scallop shells to a plate. Squeeze on fresh **lime juice**, a sprinkling of **fleur de sel**, **piment d'Espelette** (or hot paprika), and a scattering of **fresh thyme** leaves.

BACALAO CROQUETTES WITH AIOLI

Think Bar Pinotxo in Barcelona's Boqueria Market. And a note on salt preservation: a salt-cured product's shelf life is just a week, vacu-packless and preservative-free. In Arthur Kopit's play Oh Dad, Poor Dad, Mamma's Hung You in the Closet and I'm Feelin' So Sad, *Mamma kept her husband hanging in that closet for sixteen years. I wonder what she used?*

Rinse half a pound boneless **bacalao** (salt cod) in cold water until the dried salt is removed. Place in a bowl, skin side down, cover with cold water, and soak overnight, rinsing and draining at least four times. Always taste the fish before you use it to make sure it's not too salty. Poach very gently in **milk**, a **bay leaf**, and half an **onion** until the fish flakes easily. Drain, discarding the onion and bay leaf.

Shred the fish, discarding the skin and bones. Really go through it to make sure you haven't missed any tiny bones. Combine the fish in a bowl with a tablespoon of finely minced **onion**, a finely chopped clove of **garlic**, and a nice dash of **hot chili powder**. Beat an **egg** well in a separate small bowl and add just enough to make the fish mixture wet and come together. Then stir in just a little **flour** until the mixture is slightly sturdier. Stir in some finely chopped **fresh flat-leaf parsley**.

Heat a frying pan or small saucepan with about 2 or 3 inches of **peanut (groundnut) oil** (remember to keep it on the back burner for safety's sake). Test if the oil is hot enough by dropping in a smidgen of batter. It needs to begin to brown after about a minute, so adjust the heat accordingly.

Meanwhile, using two small spoons, scoop some of the mixture onto one spoon and use the other to mold into an oval shape for a quenelle, or skip this step altogether—slowly drop heaping teaspoons into the hot oil and be done with it already. Fry till golden and drain. Dip them into garlic aioli (page 150).

CARPACCIO OF BEEF, PECORINO, AND BLACK OLIVES

I love reading about the history of certain dishes. Mr. Cipriani of Harry's Bar in Venice invented the carpaccio dish and named it after the Italian painter Vittore Carpaccio. (Cipriani's famous Bellini was named after another Italian painter, Giovanni Bellini. But I wouldn't recommend having a Bellini with your carpaccio.) This is another version, and even simpler, which I adore.

Trim even the slightest bit of fat and/or gristle from a quarter to half pound **beef fillet** or **rump steak**. You can stick it in the freezer first—for about 15 minutes—to make it easier to slice, but I say just use a sharp knife and take your time.

Slice very thinly. Place the slices between two sheets of plastic wrap and bash the beef with a rolling pin until paper thin. Drape the beef in gentle folds on a large plate. Now shave paper-thin shards of a sharp **pecorino** (or an aged manchego) over the top. Scatter on some pitted and coarsely chopped **black oil-cured olives**. Drizzle an excellent **extra virgin olive oil** on top and sprinkle with **sea salt** and **cracked black pepper**.

Try this with a **Ciliegiolo del Tigullio Rosato**—a rosé made from the Ciliegiolo grape grown in Tigullio, east of Genoa.

WILD MUSHROOMS ON GRILLED CIABATTA WITH GARLIC LEMON AIOLI

A rustic, peasant-type lunch. Although I doubt peasants were ever eating this.

In a frying pan with a little **olive oil**, sweat a minced **shallot** over low heat. Add a few handfuls of sliced **wild mushrooms** and let sit—without overstirring—to let them brown slightly. Deglaze with a glug of Amontillado **sherry** till almost evaporated. Remove from the heat and mix in a sprinkling of finely chopped **fresh flat-leaf parsley**. Season well with crushed **Maldon salt** and finely ground **black pepper**. Keep warm while you grill or toast a slice or two of **ciabatta or peasant-type bread**. Drizzle the bread with a little **olive oil**, rub it with a **garlic clove**, and top slices of the bread with mushrooms. Mix a spoonful **garlic aioli** (see page 150) with a small squeeze of fresh **lemon juice** and a grating of **lemon zest** and plop on top.

PISSALADIÈRE

Do you know what? I'd always thought anchovies were the most disgusting things known to mankind. I never got it. Until I fell in love and took my first trip to the South of France, which I recommend to all (begin in Antibes). It was a quick lesson... in many things. Sardines, anchovies, the fishiest of fish, whole, heads, bones, bring 'em on... and preferably with a chilled provincial rosé. Here's a traditional French pizza.

In a small bowl, dissolve a teaspoon of **active dry yeast** in 2 tablespoons (25ml) of warm water. When completely dissolved add a tablespoon of **olive oil** and a nice pinch of **sugar**. Whisk in a small **egg**.

In another bowl, stir together ¾ cup (100g) **flour** and a pinch of **Maldon salt.** Make a well and stir in the bowl of liquid from above until incorporated. Turn onto your lightly floured counter and knead until smooth—a few minutes—adding flour as necessary. Place in a greased bowl (a drop or two of olive oil works) and keep in a warm place (I stick it in the oven). Let it rise for about an hour, until you press your finger into the dough and it springs back. If it doesn't, pretend it did.

You can also use puff pastry for the base, but I find it overkill—it's just too greasy (and I've only ever seen it prepared this way *outside* France).

Take a very large **onion**—any kind, but I'm partial to Vidalia or red. Slice it in half lengthwise, peel, and then slice each half again into very thin semicircles. In a little **olive oil** and **butter**, very very slowly cook the onions down along with a finely chopped **garlic clove** or two and a pinch of **salt** and **sugar**. We're talking the lowest possible heat here, so that you just hear the onions sizzling quietly. They should be fairly opaque in color—but tender, soft, and sweet—in about 20 minutes.

Meanwhile, open a tin or a small jar of **anchovies** and taste one to see how salty it is. You can drain them and cover them with cold **milk** for a little while to take the salt out. There are also smoky versions available, which I love.

Roll or press out the dough into a circle about half an inch thick. Place it on a baking sheet. If your dough seems too large, cut off a bit and freeze it or chuck it. Scatter the onions on top, add the drained anchovies (slice in half lengthwise if too big) in a criss-cross pattern, and sprinkle on a bunch of pitted and coarsely chopped **niçoise olives** (black, green, purple, or all three). Drizzle with a little **extra virgin olive oil**. Scatter with **fresh thyme** leaves.

Bake at 400°F (200°C) till lightly browned—about 10 to 15 minutes.

Serve with a cold tumbler of **Tavel** from the Rhône Valley.

You will now be transported to a beach in Antibes. Okay, that's a lie. This is still delicious, though.

ZUCCHINI FRITTERS WITH DILL

Thank you, Alice Waters. I changed it slightly but I think you'd be happy.

Coarsely grate a large **zucchini** into a bowl and sprinkle with **Maldon salt**. Let sit out for about 20 to 30 minutes, until all the liquid has been drawn out. Squeeze the grated zucchini with your hands until it's pretty dry, dump out the liquid, and place the zucchini back in the bowl.

Beat a small **egg** till frothy and stir about half into the zucchini, along with a minced **garlic clove** or two, some finely grated **lemon zest**, a tablespoon of **cornstarch**, and some chopped **fresh dill** (or thyme or lemon thyme). You can also add in small cubes of **cheese**, such as a soft sheep's milk—something that will melt rather quickly when you fry the fritters, so the cheese oozes out. Taste the batter before adding any additional salt and grind in some **black pepper**. The batter should be fairly thick.

Heat a pan with a few tablespoons of **olive oil** and drop in several large spoonfuls of batter. Flip the fritters when brown and sizzly and cook the other side for a few minutes. This should make between four and six fritters, depending on how big your zucchini is.

You can serve with some **Greek yogurt** mixed with a squeeze of fresh **lemon**, some chopped **chives**, and salt and pepper, if you'd like.

YELLOWTAIL SASHIMI WITH GREEN APPLE AND YUZU DIPPING SAUCE

Have you ever seen a female sushi chef? Exactly. The theory is that our hands are too warm to handle fish. Bull(cough)shite. But you might as well work quickly, ladies.

In a mortar and pestle, mix about half a tablespoon **Thai chili paste** and a few dashes of **soy sauce**. Finely grate in half a peeled **green apple** (a heaping tablespoon) and eat the rest. Then mix in a tablespoon **yuzu lime juice** (if unavailable, substitute fresh lime and lemon juice). Adjust the taste as desired. Set aside.

Sharpen your fish knife well and slice a nice portion of **sashimi-grade yellowtail** into overlapping slices onto a plate. Serve with the sauce and a glass of **cold sake**, such as a doburoku—the delicious unfiltered milky home brew.

Nice to use the sauce as a salad dressing—just add some sesame seeds and toss with fresh chicory or mixed greens.

GRILLED SARDINE PANZANELLA

Sardines=brain food: omega-3 fatty acids, vitamins D and B$_{12}$, no mercury, no PCBs, no carbohydrates, all protein, no fat, I'm not preaching but really, what's not to love here? A real delicacy.

Slice off the head and then along the tiny belly of three or four scaled **fresh sardines**. Remove the guts and rinse out the cavity gently. Trim off the tiny fin at the top with scissors. Pat dry.

Squeeze fresh **lemon juice** all over, then sprinkle with **sea salt** and **cracked black pepper**. Place on a rack set inside a pan. Broil the sardines as close to the heat as you can get them, flipping once—until the skin is completely charred and crackling (think bbq, but if you own a grill pan, use that). When they're cooked whole, they remain so much juicier.

Now place them back on your clean chopping board. Split them wide open and pull out the backbone—which will come out easily, along with the tail. Remove as many of the little bones as you want, but they're soft and completely edible, so there's no need to get crazy. Chop the fillets into nice-size bites and place in a small bowl. Tear a few slices of day-old **rustic bread** into cubes and add to the bowl. Stir in a minced **garlic clove**, very thinly sliced **red onions**, a little **sherry vinegar**, a small handful of **currants**, toasted **pine**

nuts, some **lemon zest**, a few dashes of **olive oil**, and torn **basil** and **mint leaves**. Taste to see if you need any more salt and pepper. Will be even better if you let it all sit for several minutes before placing in a small bowl and having with a chilled glass of Sicilian **Inzolia** or **Vernaccia di San Gimignano**.

VIETNAMESE SUMMER ROLLS

When I lived in Hollywood as an actor/schmactor, a friend opened a trendy Vietnamese restaurant called The Lucky Duck, on La Brea Avenue. She graciously whipped up a few of these bad boys at a dinner party in my home, from her menu at the restaurant. I'm not sure what ever happened to her, but for a party of twelve, they went in about two seconds flat. Here today, gone tomorrow, as they say in Tinseltown. Here's a version inspired by her.

PEANUT SAUCE

Boil together ¼ cup each of **sugar**, **white wine vinegar**, water, and a teaspoon of **salt**. Continue boiling until it's reduced down by half and thick and syrupy. Squeeze in juice from half a fresh **lime**, several dashes of **fish sauce**, a finely minced **red chile pepper** (or crushed red chile flakes), and a tablespoon of finely chopped **peanuts**. Set aside.

FILLING

    rice vermicelli noodles—1 or 2 cups cooked

    shrimp—a dozen or so; boil, peel, devein, and slice in half lengthwise

    cilantro, mint, and **basil**—fresh, stems removed

    rice paper—several sheets. Soak in a bowl of hot water for a minute or two—just till softened. Lay flat on a clean wet tea towel to keep from drying out.

ASSEMBLY

On a sheet of rice paper, place several shrimp one-third of the way from the bottom. Scatter on several cilantro, mint, and basil leaves. Roll up gently—careful not to tear the paper—yet tightly, just to the halfway point. Tuck in the ends and then completely roll it up (like a burrito). Cut into 1- to 3-inch slices, on the diagonal. Serve with the peanut sauce and an ice cold **Tiger beer**.

FRISÉE WITH MANCHEGO CHEESE, ROASTED MARCONA ALMONDS, AND QUINCE DRESSING

This is one of my favorites from Casa Mono restaurant in New York City. Well, possibly every dish there is my favorite. Not to be a kiss ass or anything, but this salad, which I've adapted, is inspired by their little haven of sheer perfection. I make it all the time.

Roast a few handfuls of **marcona almonds** on a baking sheet in the oven at 300°F (150°C) until lightly browned—about 10 minutes. Immediately dump half into a small bowl, drizzle on some **extra virgin olive oil** and crushed **sea salt**, and have a little snack. Let the other half of the almonds cool before you put them in a mortar and pestle and grind them down till very fine. Mix in a pinch of **pimentón de La Vera**.

In a saucepan, melt about ¼ cup **quince paste** and a few table-spoons water. Reduce to a thick syrup. Let cool a bit and whisk in a dash of **sherry vinegar** (preferably, Vinaigre de Jerez Riserva). Then slowly whisk in extra virgin olive oil—about half a cup—in a thin steady stream till thickened. Season.

Toss with some **frisée** or a variety of other crunchy greens. Sprinkle on the ground almonds and several fat shards of an aged **manchego**.

BASQUIAN LEMON SHRIMP

I could easily eat this every day of my life. The dressing on its own is magnificent—serve with hunks of fresh peasant bread or even tossed with all types of mixed greens. It's inspired by Martin Berasategui, from his eponymous three-star restaurant in San Sebastián.

In a bowl mix together the zest and juice from half a fresh **lemon**, a finely chopped **garlic clove**, two or three coarsely chopped **anchovy fillets**, a few pitted and finely chopped **oil-cured black olives**, a tablespoon of very finely chopped **red onion**, a few dashes of **sherry wine vinegar** (I like Vinaigre de Jerez Riserva, of course, but plain red wine vinegar works too), twice that amount of **extra virgin olive oil**, and a pinch of **pimentón de La Vera** for a little smoky touch (or hot paprika, but it's really not the same). Season with **sea salt** if desired.

Place six to eight large, whole jumbo **shrimp** (prawns) in boiling salted water for a few minutes, or until pink. I prefer keeping the heads on while cooking—it prevents the shrimp from becoming waterlogged and tasteless. Drain the shrimp, let them cool slightly, peel, devein, and toss into the marinade. Taste to see if a squeeze more lemon juice is needed. Let sit for an hour or two in the fridge before eating—if you can really wait that long. I can't. A big hunk of rustic bread is necessary here for hearty dunking, along with a glass of chilled **Txakoli**.

SUZIE MANNERS'S GUIDE TO MODERN ETIQUETTE

Table manners are social agreements; they are devised precisely because violence could so easily erupt at dinner...the individual's personal interest is in pleasing, placating, and not frightening or disgusting the other diners.

—MARGARET VISSER, *The Rituals of Dinner*

As I began with my amuse-bouche of a delicate chanterelle mushroom soup topped with a wispy puff of chestnut foam and one single black truffle shaving layered exquisitely in a tiny shot glass, he began with his booger. He stuck his finger up inside his nostril, slid it down, caught it, rolled it fervently between his forefinger and thumb, and flicked it to the side—all in the blink of an eye.

Wtf.

I offered him some bread. He knocked back the soup and grabbed two slices of warm sourdough bread. He scooped out a mound of butter and spread it onto one slice, like icing on a cake. Then he placed the other slice on top, squished it down, and ate it. Like a sandwich.

He wrapped his hand around his wineglass, tilted his head

straight back, opened his mouth wide—as though he were devouring a baby lamb (head first), and knocked the wine down his throat, leaving his fingerprints behind. The waiter promptly refilled his glass.

His langoustines arrived and were dismembered like this: Bite off head, suck out brains. Rip off tail, spit out shells. Pop body into mouth. Crunch down, chew. Heartily. And gulp. He then leaned over my plate—uninvited—and dug into my little birds' nests of tagliatelle with morel mushrooms. He inhaled each strand as the morels dribbled down onto the table. Then plopped them into his mouth, one by one, relishing each.

I like Neanderthals. They love to eat. Also, it's nice to feel safe, protected. For example, if we were ever burglarized in the middle of the night, I know that he'd be the one downstairs with the baseball bat—and not me. I hate the guys who cower behind you—or under the bed. You know the type. And although he did appear quite restrained in his bespoke tailored suit, it's comforting to assume he can throw a good punch.

"Did you know shellfish are bottom-feeders?" he commented.

Um, yeah, I suppose so.

"That means they eat the shit from the bottom of the sea."

Um, well yeah, I suppose so.

He was a man of few words. His voice had a remarkable resonance that gave me goose bumps. Although when he did speak, he would punctuate each thought with the tines of his fork, poking out into the air in front of him. And when he became really passionate, his fork would flail about wildly and within dangerously close range of my eyes. I had no choice but to duck and weave, like Sugar

Ray in the ring, causing a kinesthetic response with the woman behind me. I'd encroach on her invisible boundary, she'd kick my shoe.

"Would you like another bottle of wine, sir?" the waiter asked as he began to clear our plates.

"Wait one second, please. I'm not finished," my date said in slight panic. He picked up his finger bowl, removed the slice of lemon, and drank the water. "Thank you. I'd like to see the wine list again." The waiter rolled his eyes, removed the bowl, and walked off.

My date turned and asked if I'd like another bottle of wine, and I happened to notice something big and green stuck between his front teeth. I leaned over and plucked it out. Common courtesy. The table next to us whispered mockingly.

The waiter returned with the wine list. "Thanks, can you send over the smelly-A?" my date asked. The sommelier appeared. "What do you suggest?" my date asked while his left cheek slowly began to pulsate. His tongue was desperately trying to dislodge a piece of food from his back molar. He struggled as his face contorted strangely. The smelly-A peered down at my date with a snobbery I hadn't seen since the era of restaurant elitism, circa 1980.

"Perhaps you should try the '90 Cheval Blanc, sir." (This guy was going for the jugular. What a cock.)

"Nah, not white, I want a red."

"That is a red. Sir."

"Done," my date said quickly.

"I think that's rather indulgent," I snapped at the smelly-A.

"It's fine," my date winked.

The smelly-A grinned smugly, like a creepy Alan Rickman

character. He went into the back and triumphantly gave our waiter a quick high-five.

The caramelized baby squab stuffed with foie gras arrived and was a subtle showstopper. He dug right in—never unnerved by anything. He tore off its leg and nestled tenderly into its flesh. His lips glistened as he brought each finger up to his mouth—licking each with unrestrained primitive sucking noises. He grinned. A Cheshire cat grin.

"And these squab. They're pigeons, right?"

Well, baby pigeons, actually.

"So, are they, like, hunted down in Central Park?" he chuckled. "They eat everything, y'know. Bottom-feeders. One time, one shit on my head." He took a bite of his creamy polenta. "I thought I'd take a nice walk down Fifth, along the park. But I was basically dodging pigeon poop and horse shit the whole way." Just then, he took his napkin, placed it over his mouth, and removed something. Something large. Then placed the napkin back on his lap, I thought. He took another slug of wine and swirled it around his mouth, squab remnants and grease left all over the glass.

The couple behind me stood up preparing to leave. As they passed our table, they rolled their eyes with . . . yep, again, a snobbery last witnessed in 1982.

After crumbing our table and flittering around us (it was very messy), the waiter decided the linen had to be changed. He turned away in haste and within one second, completely wiped out on the floor. It was an acrobatic tumble so brilliantly executed, I thought it was a stunt. Two busboys came running over to help him up. Just next to one foot was a two-inch piece of chewed gristly gray matter with a thin trail of grease leading up to our table. My date looked away. They swept it up.

I slashed into the warm and molten Valrhona chocolate fondant. It oozed layers of hazelnut and coffee swirls with the creamiest and freshest scoop of vanilla bean ice cream quietly nestled alongside. I almost cried, I swear it was that good. We both sipped a little Sassicaia grappa, the perfect firewater digestif.

The waiter returned and hastily placed the check in the middle of the table. Unprompted. He stood directly behind us, arms crossed, waiting. You would have thought it was the end of the night and he just wanted to close out his station. Nope.

So I picked up the dessert plate, licked up the remnants, knocked back the lovely amber-colored eau-de-vie, and wiped my mouth—with the back of my hand. This had no effect on anyone, really. I also tried to burp but nothing came out. I looked like an idiot while my date just smiled, nervously.

When you're with a dining partner who is lacking in etiquette, you may want to opt for inclusivity rather than being a pretentious twat. In other words, if you can't beat 'em, join 'em. And if appropriate, you may want to teach them at some point—or just give them this chapter. But if you're the culprit (you know who you are), here are a few recipes for some tricky foods to practice eating at home, preferably in front of a mirror.

Your friend,
Suzie Manners xx

BREAD

HOMEMADE PARKER HOUSE ROLLS

I love these little guys. It's the Entenmann's store-bought classic baked right in your own oven. There's no kneading, and the rising time is minimal. I know twelve rolls are a lot in one sitting, but there was no way around it and they're just too good. I'm very sorry.

Mix together 1½ cups (210g) **bread flour,** 1½ tablespoons **sugar,** and a pinch of **sea salt** in a bowl.

In another bowl, dissolve one package of **active dry yeast** into half a cup (125ml) warm **milk.** Mix in 3 tablespoons **olive oil,** one **egg,** and one **egg yolk.** Combine the two bowls, mix well, and set aside for half an hour.

Butter a standard cake pan, casserole dish, or whatever you have that's about that size. Divide the dough into twelve even pieces and roll into balls. You may need a little more flour because they'll be sticky. Arrange them in the pan and set aside to rise again for about an hour.

Bake at 350°F (180°C) for 25 to 30 minutes, until deep golden brown. Remove, pour some melted **butter** on top, and sprinkle with **fleur de sel.**

HOW TO EAT: Ever heard the expression "break bread"? There's a reason. Aside from the centuries-old significance of its meaning, it's technically what you're supposed to do. Break off bite-size pieces from your roll or slice of bread. As for the butter, take a pat or knife-ful, place it on the edge of your bread plate, and butter the pieces individually as you go along.

SOUP
CLASSIC WINTER VEGETABLE SOUP

Chop your seasonal vegetables—such as **carrots, celery, potatoes, turnips, or leeks**—into small dice of relatively the same size—a few tablespoons of each. This is not about looking all fancy and brunoised but rather about having everything cook equally so that you'll be eating sooner. Shred in a bit of **cabbage or spinach**.

In a medium saucepan, heat a few drops of **olive oil** and add about half a cup **cured bacon** cubes (use guanciale or pancetta). Sizzle till golden. Remove and drain on paper towels. To the same saucepan, add the carrots, celery, leeks, and a few smashed **garlic cloves**. Sweat gently in the bacon fat for a few minutes. Cover the vegetables twice as high with **chicken or vegetable stock** (or just water). Then add the potatoes, turnips, cabbage, and finely chopped **fresh rosemary, thyme**, and/or **oregano** and let simmer gently for 15 to 20 minutes, until the vegetables are tender. Taste one to check.

At this point, you can add a peeled and roughly diced **tomato** (or two). Season with **Maldon salt** and ground **white pepper**.

Pour into a warmed soup bowl (wash with scalding hot water, then dry), drizzle a little **olive oil** on top, and shave on paper-thin slices of **pecorino or parmigiano. Manchego** is also lovely with this.

SPRINGTIME SOUP

Follow the same method using spring vegetables such as **green beans**, **Jerusalem artichokes**, **peas**, **sliced mushrooms**, or whatever looks good. If you'd like to skip the tomatoes, add a spoonful of **butter** for more flavor and some finely chopped spring herbs (**chervil**, **basil**, **dill**, and so on) at the very end. And the **cheese.**

Serve with warm and buttery Parker House rolls (page 120) and a glass of **Fino sherry**.

HOW TO EAT: Using a soupspoon, always spoon away from yourself. Why? No idea, just do it. Keep the noise level down too. And don't lick your fingers after each spoonful. (I swear I've seen this. I've seen it all, my friend.) For the last drops, tilt the bowl toward yourself and spoon it up. Of course, in Japanese restaurants, it's perfectly acceptable to pick up your bowl of miso soup and drink it.

SPAGHETTI (OR ANY LONG PASTA)
PASTA ALLA BOTTARGA

This is my ultimate quickie. A Sardinian classic. Bottarga is a delicacy so extraordinary that it pretty much transforms you into one big erogenous zone. It'll make you shudder at the faintest taste, its enigmatic allure transporting you to someplace magical (the beach?). Bottarga. *Indulge in its mystique. Certain restrictions apply.*

Cook a good handful of **spaghetti** till it has a nice bite and reserve a cup of pasta water. Set aside. Return the same saucepan to the heat, add a little **olive oil**, and sweat a finely chopped **garlic clove** or two. Add half a cup of the pasta water, a spoonful or two of **butter**, a few squeezes of fresh **lemon juice**, and lots of freshly shaved **bottarga di muggine** (just peel it back as you use it). Return the pasta to the pot and heat your creamy decadence through. Add more pasta water if necessary for more creaminess. Season with a hint of crushed **Maldon salt** and **cracked black pepper** and stir in some finely chopped **fresh flat-leaf parsley**.

Pour into a bowl and grate on more bottarga. Serve with a few sheets of warmed *carta musica*[†] alongside and a glass of a chilled local Sardinian **Vermentino**, and you're laughin'.

HOW TO EAT: A fork only, please. Pull forward a small quantity of pasta. Then turn the fork straight down and twizzle the pasta around its tines into a small bundle. That's really it. No spoons. No knives.

[†] Sardinian flatbread: warm in the oven, drizzle with olive oil, and sprinkle with crushed sea salt. To order, go to Sources, page 217.

TAGLIATELLE WITH BLACK TRUFFLES

What's the deal with truffles? Such a fuss already. They're really just the arboreal equivalent of foot fungus. Don't you like foot fungus? Shall I try and persuade you otherwise? If you can get past the whole burned-out overdone hoopla that surrounds them, you can then start over. They're cute. They're fragrant as hell, seasonal, quirky, and if prepared correctly—which doesn't take much—interestingly tasty. But it's all in their smell, which for me is intoxicating. And isn't that just taste, anyway? But I'll save the polemics for another time. Jump-start your new attitude with this:

Cook a good handful of **tagliatelle**. Reserve a cup of the cooking water. Meanwhile, sweat a finely chopped **garlic clove** or two in **olive oil**. Add several tablespoons of the reserved **pasta water**, a spoonful of **butter**, and grated **parmigiano, pecorino, or grana padano** cheese. Heat through gently for a minute, until the cheese and butter have melted. Toss in the tagliatelle and gently heat through. Remove from the heat. Now take out that little **black truffle** nugget that's been sniffed out of the woods by some adorable girlie pig, harvested, and carefully shipped with tender loving care. Slice the truffle as thinly as humanly possible and toss as much as you'd like into the pasta. Season with **Maldon salt** and **cracked black pepper**.

Mound onto a plate. You can also get really carried away with a drizzle of **truffle oil** if you'd like. No harm in that.

Again, white or red? There are no rules. An earthy white Burgundy such as **Chablis** or from the Rhône Valley such as **Hermitage Blanc or Crozes Hermitage**. Refer to the red suggestions in Three-Cheese Ravioli, page 60.

LITTLE BONY BIRDS
GRILLED SPATCHCOCKED SPICED QUAIL

Little birds are a pain in the ass to eat, particularly when you're starving. But they're tasty as heck.

Spatchcock a quail, squab, partridge, grouse, woodcock—whatever little bird is in season. Here's what you do:

With the breast down on a chopping board, use a very sharp small knife or heavy scissors to cut along each side of the backbone and remove it. Cut off the wing tips. Open the bird up and wash thoroughly in cold water, removing any bits of innards. Take out the wishbone, grab the lucky side, and make a wish. It will come true, I swear. Now open up the little bird and place it with the breast down again. Press your hand down firmly and break the breastbone. It should now lie flat.

In small bowl, mix a heaping tablespoon of **Chinese five-spice powder**, some **olive oil**, a few tablespoons of fresh **orange or tangerine juice**, a dash of **hot chili pepper** or crushed **red chile flakes**, and a few minced **garlic cloves**. Sprinkle the bird with a bit of **Maldon salt**, then rub the spice mixture all over. Place in the fridge for an hour to marinate.

Beginning with the skin side down, broil about 3 to 4 inches from the heat for a few minutes. Flip and finish it off skin side up very close to the heat so it'll be extra crispy. It's best medium-rare to medium for gamy birds. (To test: prick with a fork in the thickest part of the leg; the juices should run slightly pink.) Let rest before eating.

Serve with rice, sautéed greens, and a lovely glass of a chilled **German Riesling** (see Best Pork Chops and Applesauce, page 22).

HOW TO EAT: A messy meal indeed, but it's supposed to be. In no particular order, twist off the wings. Nibble. Twist or cut off the legs. Nibble. Use a knife and fork for the breasts. That's it. You can lick your fingers. As I said, it's a messy meal. Just refrain from loud sucking noises. And as for drinking wine with your bird, hold the glass by the stem, as you should. Thank you.

SHELLFISH

CAZUELA DE ARROZ LANGOUSTINES

I'm embracing my Spanish roots here. I really wish I had known my grandmother. Many years ago, she owned and ran a little Spanish restaurant on the Upper West Side of Manhattan named Francesca's after her. She was a one-woman show, and did everything. That poor poor woman. My mother claimed she made a daily paella. I'd imagine it to be like this:

Pan-fry a soft-cured **chorizo** sausage (dulce or picante) in a skillet till brown on all sides and bursting out of its skin. Add a little olive oil if necessary. Remove, drain on paper towels, and set aside, reserving the oil. Sweat a heaping tablespoon of minced **onion** and two minced **garlic cloves** in the chorizo oil. Add two medium **tomatoes**, diced, and a pinch of **Maldon salt** and gently cook until the tomatoes break down and it all becomes a rich sauce. This is your *sofrito*. (At this point, you can just pick out the tomato skins.) Add a half to three-quarters cup **Bomba or Calasperra rice** and stir to coat well. Add a cup of fresh **fish or chicken stock**, a glug of a **sherry**, a pinch of **saffron** threads, a dash of **hot chili powder**, and the browned chorizo, sliced, and let simmer a minute. It's a good time now to taste it and season lightly with a dash of the sea salt and **black pepper**, if necessary.

Place three or four fresh whole **langoustines** facedown in the pan. Do not stir, and let the rice slowly absorb the gently simmering liquid. Add more stock, as necessary (you'll probably use about 1½ to 2 cups per half a cup rice), shaking the pan lightly so the rice doesn't stick. When the rice seems to swell nicely, turn the langoustines over. Scatter in a handful of fresh or frozen **peas** and some roughly chopped **fresh flat-leaf parsley**. Cook for another 5 to 10 minutes, till the rice is tender and the langoustines are pale pink. Serve with half a fresh **lemon**.

Try with a Spanish rosé, such as a **Rioja Vina Tondonia Rosé Gran Riserva**. The softer rose petal quality works nicely with the saffron and chorizo. This one in particular needs to be opened way in advance.

HOW TO EAT: Expect to dig in and get messy. Shellfish cooked whole are always messy. Langoustines sometimes squirt when you twist off their heads. With that said, using both hands, twist off its head. Then peel off the shell from its body. Eat up until the shell of the tail. It's perfectly fine to suck—just refrain from making loud noises. Do I have to say this again?

EAT YOUR GREENS!
THREE WAYS

FIRST

Over low heat, sweat a few chopped **garlic cloves** and a finely minced **green chile pepper.** Add many handfuls of **watercress, dandelion greens,** or any combination of seasonal hearty **dark-leafed greens** that you'd like to jazz up. Turn up the heat and sauté till just wilted. Remove from the heat and stir in a touch of **sesame oil** and **soy sauce.**

SECOND

Macerate a tablespoon or two of **currants** in hot water. Pan-fry a handful of **pignoli nuts** in **olive oil.** Add many handfuls of **dark greens** and again, stir till wilted. Drain the currants and stir in. Season with a little **red wine vinegar,** a dash more **olive oil,** and **salt** and **pepper.**

THIRD

Wash about five or six large handfuls of fresh **spinach** very well. (If it's from a market, just place it in a big bowl of cold water and all the dirt will sink to the bottom. Drain and repeat this several times or until you bite into a leaf and it no longer has that gritty, nails-down-a-chalkboard feel, which is the worst.) Cut off the stems and chop it roughly. Pile into a metal colander and place it over a medium pot of boiling water (2 to 3 inches of water will do). Cover with a lid to steam the spinach until it's just wilted—a minute or two, max. I like to preserve the vitamins. By the way, this is my makeshift steamer method. Remove the colander, rinse the spinach quickly with cold water—to stop it from cooking any further and to keep it bright and green—then use your hands to squeeze out the water.

In a frying pan over low heat, sweat a teaspoon of a finely chopped **shallot** or **garlic** in a tablespoon of melted **butter** till soft. Add a tablespoon of **flour** and whisk till it starts to bubble. Add in ¾ cup (about 175ml) cold **milk** and continue whisking until the béchamel has thickened. Season with a grating of **fresh nutmeg, Maldon salt**, and **white pepper**. Squeeze out any remaining liquid from the spinach before adding to the béchamel and heating the whole thing through.

Voilà, creamed spinach.

HOW TO EAT: Greens get stuck between your teeth, that's life. But if your dining partner doesn't make you aware of it, that's evil. Toothpicks at the table are equivalent to dental floss at the table. Excuse yourself and deal with it in the restroom.

JUST MESSY
A BIG OL' BURGER

I love watching people eat in public. It's fascinating. This is inspired by one of the many delectable stands in Borough Market, London.

For a great hamburger, it's all about the meat. **Short rib**, **sirloin**, **brisket**, **chuck**, **filet**, **wagyu** . . . the combination is your choice. But here's the catch. You need to befriend your butcher. Because unless you're giving your butcher special favors on the side, a portion for one won't be worth his or his meat grinder's time. It's called discrimination. But it's also not that economical because some will get left behind in the grinder's tube. So either buy enough meat and freeze your already-made burgers or simply hand-chop (a bonus for one serving but too much effort for two or more), which works like this:

Decide on what combo of meats you'd like to try. Perhaps a **short rib** and **chuck** combo? I'd say nine or ten ounces (250g/300g) of meat in a 2:1 ratio for a large to extra-large burger. The short rib requires some minor butchery—about half is fat and bone and will be discarded—so adjust. The ground chuck is pretty easy to find.

Separate the two layers of meat on the short rib (you can ask your butcher to cut away the bone), and trim away all the fat, muscle, and tendons—pretty much anything you wouldn't want to eat. With a very sharp and heavy knife, cut the meat into cubes, then mince finely and place in bowl with the chuck. Add a big pinch of **Maldon salt** and mix together well. Shape it into a hefty patty.

To a hot frying pan, add a little **oil** (any kind) and a little **butter**. Fry the burger, continually flipping, basting with the butter, and keeping the juices flowing. It'll be perfectly fragile, so you can almost see straight through as it oozes to a medium rare. Remove and make sure you let it rest for a good five minutes before placing it on top of a thick slice of fresh **brioche** and plopping on **mustard, ketchup, and mayo,** thinly sliced **dill pickles, red onions, tomatoes,** and a large **lettuce** leaf or two. Slam shut with another thick slice of brioche.

Wine: an old school **Barbera** from Piedmont.

Beer: **Any**.

Milkshake: **Chocolate**.

Let a pint of Häagen-Dazs **chocolate ice cream** soften ever so slightly. Scoop out half and into a glass. Stir in just a little icy cold **milk**, so it's thick and lusty. If it's too melted, skip the milk and drink it straight (out of the carton).

HOW TO EAT: Using both hands to hold each side of burger, dive in and take the largest bite you can possibly fit into your mouth. Do so with hedonistic fervor and abandonment. Let the juices drip down your arms. Only, please wipe your mouth with a napkin after each bite. Using your tongue, like a dog, to clean the sides of your mouth is not becoming on anyone. No one wants to catch glimpses of your filthy tongue. And as I said before, licking and sucking your fingers when nibbling on bones is *perfectly acceptable—and necessary* (see Little Bony Birds, page 128). But in this case, and most others, it's not a good look. Hint: if your dining companion is constantly looking away, it may be a sign that you're being offensive. But if he's also a farm animal, then you'll both be in full glory. Oink.

BRUNCH: WHY?

L'enfer, c'est les autres. (Hell is other people.)
—JEAN-PAUL SARTRE, *No Exit*

There's something quietly exciting about breakfast. After a satisfying morning orgasm, nothing else quite gets my day going. But it absolutely must be spent in serenity. Alone or not. This is the time when I'm secretly plotting to rule the world, and anything remotely disquieting (the very efficient leaf blower man, the glass recycling truck, the pigeons humping on my windowsill) becomes an assault on my consciousness (not to mention my plans).

I guess that's why I just don't get brunch. The only way I can make it through one is if I'm up at the crack of dawn and have an entire morning and breakfast to myself. But on a Sunday? What kind of control freak workaholic people-pleasing whack job would do that? You can see your friends for dinner.

So, this is how it goes. I set aside my misanthropic tendencies and agree to a Sunday brunch out. The invitation is a month in advance—to accommodate everyone (else's) psychotically busy life. (Whatever happened to spontaneity?) As soon as I agree, I know my weekend is already ruined. I start thinking the night before about how I have to wake up at a ridiculously early hour to pull myself together and become the friendly, outgoing person that people see me as. So, of course I have a restless sleep. I mean, setting my alarm clock on a Saturday night? That's just sick.

Of course, I miss the alarm. In between shaky sips of scalding tea and an unusually cold shower, I manage to make it out the door and arrive at the restaurant just on time.

Of course, everyone else is late. "Sorry, but we can't seat you until the rest of your party has arrived," the hostess croaks. She seems nice enough and I dutifully take a seat at the empty bar and ask the bartender for a cup of tea.

Fifteen minutes later, she brings a teapot over. And a cup. "Um, can I have some sugar, please—and milk? Just heated a bit—that would be great. Thank you so much." I detect a slight scowl. She makes an about-face, barks at a waitress on the floor, and continues tending to the dupes that are slowly flooding her service area.

I wait patiently as a crescendo of chaos intensifies around me. Waiters begin stomping past—the vibrations of their footsteps resound in my empty stomach; strollers of screaming kids pile in, air kisses, hostility, crashing glasses, mops. It's Cirque du Soleil in hell, but without the fire jugglers.

I put my head down and place my hands around my teapot, which is now lukewarm. I catch another waiter's eye and smile as I signal for milk and sugar. I'm trying my best. He nods and walks off. The bartender now returns with a small porcelain sugar bowl. "Thank you. And the milk? . . . Please?" Another scowl, and she barks at the waitress again. I lift the cover off the bowl only to find pink and blue packets of Sweet'N Low and NutraSweet, which are non-negotiable for me. The bartender then returns with the milk, which is icy. "Thanks. Listen, it's probably too much to ask, but this milk is ice cold, and the tea is now tepid. Would it be possible to either have a new pot of hot tea or just some really hot milk? And, do you have any sugar. Real sugar?" I instinctively duck, assuming she's about to throw the teapot at my head. She hates me.

Then the waiter I motioned to earlier hobbles over with milk and sugar. I thank him. My phone begins beeping wildly as a succession of texts come through: "We're just on our way now, no taxis . . ." "Petie's practice is running late . . ." "Isabella woke up with a fever . . ." "Moving slowly, am sooo hungover . . ."

My tea is now cold. Ice cold. And all I seem to hear is the cacophonic background music: *"Are you absolutely sure this is decaf? . . . Do you have soy milk? . . . I said no butter on my toast! . . . You forgot the syrup . . . ketchup . . . I asked for no ice in my juice . . . Lower the music . . . Do you have a high chair? . . . Egg whites only . . . raspberry, not marmalade . . . I'm allergic . . . I'm intolerant . . . I'm stupid . . ."*

"We're going to give away your table if your friends aren't here in the next two minutes. As you can see, we have a mob waiting outside and we've held your table for over twenty-five minutes." I look out the window, and sure enough, a mob is forming on the street. It crosses my mind that hundred-dollar bills or some other reward is being granted upon entry, and the hostess has excluded my insurmountably demanding self.

"I know, I'm so sorry. I just got their texts and they'll all be here any minute." I cringe.

The tea is not happening. I'm also starved. I knew I should have grabbed a croissant on the way. I hunch over and shield myself with the menu from the hostess and the bartender, who are now both scowling at me. Far too much drama for a Sunday.

The hostess walks back over to me. "Okay, I'm really sorry, but I have to give up your table. Settle up at the bar before you leave, please. And just to let you know, we'll be charging the credit card under the reservation name fifty dollars. That's our policy. Sorry."

I just didn't have it in me to argue, complain, fight. You have to choose your battles in this city, and frankly, this was a losing one. And it's far too early. Besides, I love paying six bucks for a lousy pot of tea I never drank. The bartender scowls but I smile. I know it's my last Sunday brunch out. Ever. I leave her a twenty and skip out the door.

BLUEBERRY PANCAKES

The good old American kind.

Open a bottle of **maple syrup** (keeping the loosened lid on), place it in a small pan of water, and heat gently. Keep it in hot water until ready to use.

Sift or stir together (depending on how motivated you are) half a cup (70g) **flour**, half a teaspoon **baking powder**, ¼ teaspoon **baking soda**, a tablespoon **sugar**, and a tiny pinch of **salt**.

In another bowl, pour in half a cup (125ml) **milk** and squeeze in a spoonful of fresh **lemon juice** (to make fresh buttermilk). Beat in an **egg yolk** and a teaspoon of **vanilla extract** or scrape in half a vanilla bean. Reserve the **egg white.** Whisk the wet ingredients into the dry just until the lumps are gone. Easy does it here.

In one last bowl, whisk the **egg white** until soft peaks form. Very gently fold it into the batter. If you overmix the batter, your pancakes will turn out like lead Frisbees.

Melt a tablespoon or two of **butter** in a frying pan. When it's bubbly, make two pancakes by pouring in a few tablespoons of pancake batter for each. Sprinkle on a bunch of fat fresh **blueberries**. When the pancakes are bubbly, flip and cook for another minute or two. Serve with the warm maple syrup. Repeat. You're good for four of these.

In the winter, grate a peeled apple into the batter and add a good dash of cinnamon before frying.

SCRAMBLED EGGS

Just a few minutes longer than it takes to prepare your old boring scrambled eggs and you'll have a little plate of pure perfection for yourself.

Crack three of the best and freshest **eggs** you can find into a sieve that has been placed over the top pan of a double boiler. Whisk well. Using a rubber spatula, sieve the eggs through, leaving the yuck part of the albumen behind. Now bring the water to a gentle simmer as you stir the eggs vigorously with a wooden spoon. When they begin to thicken, add a tablespoon or two each of **cream** and **butter**, a good sprinkling of **Maldon salt**, and some freshly ground **white pepper**. Some finely chopped **chives** wouldn't hurt either. Within minutes, it'll become a beautiful creamy concoction of the most delicately soft and tiniest of curds that you'll heap up and serve alongside a thick slice of toasted brioche. I know I'm being a complete cheeseball, but it really doesn't get any better than this.

All of the brunch dishes go nicely with a **Moscato d'Asti**, which is light and fizzy and has a natural sweetness. Or better:

A BLOODY MARY

Fill a glass halfway with ice and pour in a few shots of a fancy **vodka**. Fill any space left in the glass with **tomato juice**, freshly grated **horseradish**, a dash of **Tabasco**, and a splash of **Worcestershire**. Stick in a huge, chilled, and crisp **celery** stalk—leaves intact—and stir well using the stalk end.

HOME-CURED GRAVLAX WITH BAGELS AND CREAM CHEESE

Saturday (6½-minute prep)

Place a half- to three-quarter-pound fillet of **wild salmon** with skin in a shallow dish. (Make sure it's a nice fat piece and not an end. You'll get bigger slices later on.) Remove any pin bones. In a mortar and pestle, grind a tablespoon of **Maldon or kosher salt**, a tablespoon of **sugar**, three **white peppercorns**, and two **juniper berries**. Rub all over the salmon. Place a few stems of **dill** and a little grated **lemon zest** on the bottom of a small casserole dish and add the salmon, skin side up. Pour a tablespoon of **gin** over the top. Cover loosely with plastic and place a plate on top, and then something heavy to compress it—such as a can or two of tomatoes, or a bag of rocks. Place in the fridge and allow to cure for twenty-four hours. About twelve hours in, if you can remember to drain it once and flip it over, even better.

Sunday (6-minute-20-second finish)

Drain and wipe the cure mixture off the fillet. Using your sharpest knife, cut thin slices through the fillet, but not through the skin at the bottom. If the fillet comes to a slight peak at the center, begin at the center and slice outward at a 45-degree angle. Repeat with the other side. For a Swedish/Jewish combo, slice a **bagel** in half—pumpernickel is nice—thickly spread on some **cream cheese**, layer on the gravlax, and top with very thinly sliced **red onion**.

The variations here are endless: begin with your basic brine recipe (sugar, salt, and pepper) and experiment with brown or muscovado sugar or even pomegranate molasses; different herbs such as parsley, basil, coriander, even thyme; or with booze such as vodka or tequila. Try a soy sauce and sake combo; grated beet and lime zest combo . . . etc., etc. It's all been done before, and the results will vary greatly. Just remember, even though you may think you need more, the impact of just a single stem of an herb will make a noticeable difference in taste. It's all pretty delicate, and too much of something or too many varieties will be overpowering. Once I tried a huge bunch of mint with several other herbs, a hefty shot of gin, and a handful of cracked white peppercorns and it was disgusting. Have fun!

FRIED DUCK EGG WITH GUANCIALE AND TOAST

I mean this is just stupidly perfect: smoky, salty, garlicky, lemony, and that egg!—it's like a cartoonish sunrise. And with a hunk of warm toast to slather it up? Just stupid. And for the hell of it, go the extra step and slice white or black truffles over it all. Gluttony at its best. Damn.

Thinly slice some **guanciale** and fry till crisp. Drain and set aside. In the same hot pan, crack a **duck egg** or two into the bacon fat (of course if it's burned, wipe it out and melt a little butter) and fry sunny side up for a minute or two longer than you would a regular chicken egg. While they're cooking, hand-cut a few slices of **Poilâne or hearty peasant bread**. Toast and drizzle with **olive oil**. Toss a handful of **frisée or other mixed greens** with a little **garlic aioli** (see page 150). Mound onto a plate, place the egg on top, scatter on the guanciale, and stack the toast on the side.

FRITTATA CON DELLE ERBE

A fancy name for a simple dish.

Finely chop some **fresh chives, dill,** and **chervil**. Whisk two **egg whites** and two **whole eggs** together until really frothy. Add in the herbs, a little **Maldon salt,** and some **white pepper**. Heat **olive oil** in a small omelet or frying pan and add the eggs. I really do like a few dollops of **goat cheese** here, but it's up to you. With a rubber spatula, gently lift along edges, tilting the pan so that the uncooked part runs down to the bottom. Flip the frittata over onto a large plate the same size, then slide back into the pan to cook other side. The whole thing should be puffed and golden. Slide onto a plate and serve with toast and sausages.

WARM BEIGNETS

Breakfast of Champions. And, I might add, better than Krispy Kremes.

You're pretty much making pâte à choux here. In saucepan, heat half a cup of water, ¼ cup strained, fresh **orange juice**, lots of fresh **lemon zest**, a generous squeeze of fresh **lemon juice**, 4 tablespoons (60g) **butter**, a pinch of **salt**, and a tablespoon of **sugar**. Bring to a boil. Remove from heat and stir in half a cup (70g) **flour**. Beat well, letting the heat cook out the flour—a few minutes. Remove from heat and let cool for a minute. Add two **eggs**, one at a time (try not to let them touch the bottom of the saucepan or they may scramble), beating vigorously with a wooden spoon till glossy and ribbony.

In 2 inches of hot **peanut (groundnut) oil**, spoon in heaping teaspoonfuls (test one first—it should brown within 4 to 5 minutes) and fry until deep golden brown. When you take a bite, it should be extraordinarily wispy, light, and lovely and literally melt in your mouth. Drain on paper towels.

Mix half a cup of sifted **confectioners' sugar (icing sugar)** with a few drops of **milk or cream** and half a scraped **vanilla bean** in a small bowl until silky and fairly thick. Drizzle the icing over the beignets *or* put a few spoonfuls of **granulated sugar** on a plate and stir in a few dashes of **cinnamon**. Roll the warm beignets all around to coat well. By the way, Krispy Kremes are good only when they're warm and straight out of that massive industrial oven—so when you buy them, it is imperative that your timing is right. Otherwise, they're just average.

Or pile up warm beignets in a bowl and dip them into spoonfuls of . . .

WARM BERRY JAM

Place a cup of your favorite **berries** in a small saucepan with two tablespoons of **sugar or honey**, a few tablespoons of water, and a small squeeze of **lemon**. Bring to a boil, mash down slightly with fork, and reduce down slowly till thick.

BLT ON TOASTED BRIOCHE
WITH GARLIC AIOLI

In a mortar and pestle, mash up a **garlic clove** or two (or roasted garlic, page 19), an equal amount of **lemon zest**, and a squeeze of **lemon juice**. Scrape into a small bowl and beat in a very small **egg yolk**. Slowly drizzle half **olive oil** and half **grapeseed oil** (about half a cup in total) into the center in a thin steady stream and whisk away until it emulsifies into a thick aioli. Season with **salt** and **white pepper**. Set aside.

Fry up several slabs of thickly cut **smoked bacon**. While they're cooking, toast two slices of **brioche**, thickly slice a **tomato**, and wash and dry some **greens** of your choice. Drain bacon on a paper towel.

Now make up your sandwich.

SIXTIES GRANOLA

I'm not a big granola fan, I must say. But sometimes I need to look after a lover who may not always want decadent goose fat with extra salt for breakfast. So I do, begrudgingly, keep a large mason jar of this in the fridge for him, so he stays fit and healthy (for me).

Mix together a handful of each in a bowl: **flaxseeds**, **hemp seeds**, **raw oatmeal**, **goji berries**, **currants or golden raisins**, **raw almonds**, **walnuts**, **sunflower seeds**, and **pumpkin seeds**.

Add some melted **butter** (I can't help myself) and lots of **agave nectar or honey** until the mixture starts to clump. Sprinkle in a nice dash of **cinnamon**. Store in an airtight mason jar in your fridge for years.

Known to be delicious with spoonfuls of Greek yogurt and sliced bananas.

WASTE MANAGEMENT

BECAUSE THERE'S NO SUCH THING AS LEFTOVER DESSERT

Leave the gun. Take the cannolis.

—CLEMENZA, *The Godfather*

I hate wasting food. When I waitressed, the carnage at the end of the shift—particularly for those massive catering events—was catastrophic. Was it just improper planning on the kitchen's part? You never know. But as we were breaking down, which for me meant hiding in an alley until the trucks were loaded up and ready to leave, I'd be the first to survey the remains in the kitchen to see what I could take with me. I always befriended the chefs so they'd hook me up. So, as my coworkers would break down tables, fold hundreds of chairs, collect bags of dirty linens, and carry out racks and racks of glassware, I would happily be off in a corner wrapping a tenderloin of beef, long baguettes, and an entire pastry shop of desserts.

The desserts were tricky because they were usually very perishable and cumbersome, which made them difficult to manage on the subway. But I always did. Because the food wasn't for me. I'd hand

"Okay." After working on pulled and blown sugar for weeks at a time in school, I was pretty psyched.

"Over there you'll find twenty small cast-iron pans for baby tarte tatins. Use those Comice pears in the walk-in. And the puff from the back freezer." A trainee, Kerry-Anne, promptly brought over some puff pastry in a soggy-ish package. I took a whiff.

"Um, I'm sorry, but it's wet and smells like freezer burn. I'll make some quick puff."

"Uh, good. I think Jon the Baker saved us a few loaves of brioche for bread and butter pudding. Make it Jamie-style with bananas and Bailey's. Oh, we're out of Bailey's."

"I'll use rum, macerate the raisins, and serve with a warm anglaise . . . perhaps sweetened with maple syrup?"

"There's some in dry storage outside. Can you use this desiccated coconut?"

"What if I infuse the coconut in an anglaise for ice cream and serve that with the pineapple instead, then I'll use the pear skins from the pear tartes Tatins and infuse them in the cream for a white chocolate ganache to use for baby white chocolate tarts?"

"Uh, cool."

"Too much pear?"

"We'll go through the pear tarte tatins for lunch and do the white chocolate pear tarts for dinner. Two more ideas?"

I knew I needed something really dark to offset the already fruity light-colored menu.

"Chocolate tart—but with a chocolate pâte sucrée, and the ganache will be lightened with an egg before baking and topped with a hunk of roasted nut brittle of some kind."

I wanted monochrome colors—and pictured a circle of deep brown and buttery toffee sauce on the left side of the sharp triangle of black on black tart with a shard of toasty brown brittle on the upper right side. Basic building block shapes—childlike but perfectly executed.

He smiled. We were on the same page. "Panna cottas. I want simple vanilla bean ones. The Australian mafia keep adding chiles to them. Find those damn dariole molds—the chefs keep stealing them for their mise. Use the rhubarb—roasted in simple syrup, vanilla beans, orange rinds, star anise, and black pepper. Bake some thin and crispy ginger biscuits. The plate will be assembled like this: panna cotta in the center, chopped rhubarb confit—or marmellata—to the left, a splash of grappa, and smashed ginger biscuits to the right. One dip of panna cotta, dip in marmellata, and dip in biscuits. Prince Charles loved it. Those blood oranges and Amalfi lemons need to get used for sorbets. They're some recipes in that black file, top shelf if you need them. Cheers, Miss America."

That took about ten minutes. And I was off. The name stuck, unfortunately.

In this job, the waste wasn't too severe but only because I measured my ingredients with accuracy and shut the bushwhacking Aussie chefs up by feeding them my confections. Or threatening them with my knife. Oops, was that out loud?

The rigidity of precise measurements (yawn) in pastry making is imperative. Tricky for one serving? Not for these recipes. (But a leftover dessert is an oxymoron.)

ONE BIG PROFITEROLE

Pay attention here because I want you to get this right. The whole thing is so quick, you won't even know what happened. This is a winner, hands down.

For the choux: in a small saucepan boil together a quarter cup (60ml) water and 2 tablespoons (exactly 25g here) **butter**, a pinch of **salt**, and a pinch of **sugar**.

Take the pan off the heat and using a wooden spoon, vigorously stir in ¼ cup (35g) **flour** until the dough comes together and off the sides of the pan. Then, return the pan over low heat and continue stirring until the choux is dry and the flour cooks out a bit—about 30 seconds. Remove from the heat once again and place the choux into a medium bowl (keep the saucepan close by). Using the wooden spoon, stir in one **egg** and mix vigorously. This stage is weird. Because there's such a tiny amount, we need to do this off the heat at first; otherwise, as soon as that egg hits any part of the saucepan, you'll have scrambled egg choux. So, continue stirring. The mixture will look like slithery scraps of dough, but then chemistry takes over. Return the choux to the pan (off the heat) and stir wildly. The remaining heat from the pan will bring this mixture together into a beautifully glossy paste. I like how that happens.

Using a spoon, scoop up a smooth and heaping mound of choux pastry—dividing the mixture into three lovely little profiteroles

(I lied about just one; it's never worked—too doughy and too eggy) and onto a buttered baking sheet. Bake at 325°F (170°C) for 15 to 20 minutes, till golden and puffy.

Meanwhile, *make the chocolate sauce:* combine 2 tablespoons (30g) of your best **70 percent dark chocolate**, finely chopped, a quarter cup **water**, 2 tablespoons (30g) **crème fraîche or light cream**, and a tablespoon (15g) **sugar** in a saucepan and slowly simmer till creamy and thick.

Cut off the top third of each profiterole, place a small scoop of **vanilla ice cream** inside, put the tops back on, and place them on a plate. Spoon the warm chocolate sauce on top. I don't do unnecessary garnishes and never understood the point of an unused mint leaf. Also, why do so many pastry chefs still insist on drawing sperm squiggles of sauce on every plate?

CRÊPES SUZETTE

I'd never had one of these until I made them for myself. I was a bit shocked. They are so frigging good.

Whisk together half a cup (125ml) **milk**, 6 tablespoons (54g) **flour**, one **egg**, a teaspoon of **sugar**, and a pinch of crushed **Maldon salt** until smooth. Set aside.

Heat a small omelet pan. Coat with a few drops of **oil** and when just smoking, pour in enough batter just to cover the bottom of the pan, tilting pan back and forth so that it coats evenly. Cook the crêpe till lightly brown on the bottom and the top is set. This is a good time to practice your flipping skills. Loosen the edges of the crêpe with a rubber spatula (we're cheating here, but let's make sure it doesn't stick), lift up the pan, tilt it forward at a 45-degree angle, and give it a good quick push up, so that the crêpe flips up into the air and drops straight back down into the pan. Don't worry, you'll have four more to practice with. Cook till golden. Remove and place on parchment and repeat with the rest of the batter.

Wipe the pan and add 3 tablespoons **sugar** and 1 teaspoon freshly squeezed **lemon juice**. Heat slowly until it begins to caramelize, then stir in half a cup (125ml) strained and freshly squeezed **orange juice**, half a **cinnamon stick**, and two whole **cloves**. Continue stirring until the sugar has re-melted and the sauce is smooth. Add 2 tablespoons **Grand Marnier or Cointreau** and, over high heat, reduce it down until slightly thickened. Finish with one or two chunks of **butter** and stir until the sauce is looking succulent, which it will be.

Add a crêpe to the pan and bathe it in the sauce. Fold it in half, then in half again, setting it aside in the pan. Repeat with one or two more crêpes. Move them to one side of the pan, remove from heat, and pour a small glug of **cognac** into the open side of the pan. Standing back as far as possible, ignite the cognac with a match. Let the sauce catch fire and burn itself out. It's not as dramatic as you think. Arrange the crêpes back into the sauce (spoon out a bit, if too much) and sprinkle on a handful of toasted **hazelnuts**, a few **orange segments**, and finely grated **orange zest**, if you'd like. Eat them warm in the pan with a fork.

FRESH PINEAPPLE TARTE TATIN

This is an elegant little number—not too sweet, with hints of savory. Besides using apples and pears, try using another fruit. Be creative. Bananas work too, just skip the first step, caramelize them, and, oh never mind, that's a whole different recipe altogether. Another time.

Place a small fresh **pineapple** on its side and slice off the top. Cut it in half horizontally, take the bottom half, wrap it up, place in the fridge, and eat it for breakfast. Now stand the top half upright and work your way around the pineapple, slicing the skin off and discarding. Then slice down half-inch-thick rectangles, creating four sides, and leaving the core intact, which you can suck on, then discard. Now slice the rectangles into same-size squares—no larger than 3 by 3 inches—and place the slices in a saucepan. Cover with water and add a **star anise**, a little **sugar**, four or five **black peppercorns**, a **vanilla bean**, scraped and with the pod, and an **orange rind**, if you have it. Bring to a boil, reduce the heat, and simmer very gently for 10 minutes, or just until soft. Set aside.

Have one or two small (4-inch) cast-iron skillets close by. In a stainless steel frying pan, heat half a cup (100g) **sugar** over very low heat. As the sugar begins to melt, gently shake the pan back and forth, careful not to heat it too quickly. When it's completely melted and becomes an amber color (it will deepen in color while baking), add a tablespoon of **butter** and stir in until melted. Immediately pour a quarter to half an inch of the caramel into your cast-iron skillet(s). Throw the frying pan into hot soapy water. Now.

Remove the pineapple slices and drain, reserving the liquid. Layer the slices over the caramel, overlapping in a pattern of your choice but no more than two layers high. Using defrosted and prepared **puff pastry**, cut into a circle so it's slightly larger than the skillet and lay it over the pineapple. Gently press the edges in.

Place on a baking sheet and bake at 400°F (200°C) for about 15 minutes, until it's a golden and bubbly puff. Set aside to cool for a few minutes.

Strain the pineapple liquid and pour it back into the saucepan. Add a small shot of rum and reduce it down over high heat until it's thick and syrupy.

Flip the tarte tatin over onto a plate and serve with a spoonful of **vanilla ice cream**, plain **mascarpone or crème fraîche**, and a drizzle of the rum syrup.

Go to page 203 to find a few uses for that tub of mascarpone or crème fraîche.

CAKE

This cake improves with age, like myself. And yes, I know, you can add all kinds of things to the batter—orange zest, raisins, rosemary … tires—but I like it plain. Leave me alone. Give me my rum.

Beat a quarter pound (115g) really soft unsalted **butter** in a bowl until it is similar in creaminess to a ridiculously expensive face cream—think Crème de la Mer. Mix in 1 cup (200g) **sugar**, then 2 cups (230g) **ground almonds**. Add five **eggs**, incorporating each one at a time. Turn into a buttered and floured mold, loaf pan, or whatever seems appropriate and bake at 325°F (170°C) until the aromas of a decadent little Parisian bakery have drifted through your home—about 45 to 55 minutes. Stick a knife in the cake—it should come out clean. Now it really needs to cool before devouring, but before it does, pour a glass of an aged **rum** for yourself, such as a twenty-three-year-old Ron Zacapa Centenario, then pour half down that long crack in the middle of the cake. Just like your granny used to do.

LEMON-LIME GELATO

A lovely little palate cleanser.

In a saucepan, stir together a quarter cup (60ml) freshly squeezed **lemon juice** and its **zest**, a quarter cup freshly squeezed **lime juice** and its **zest**, and a half cup (100g) **sugar**. Simmer for a few minutes, until the sugar has dissolved. Taste and add more sugar if you'd like. Strain and let cool down in the fridge.

Stir in half a cup (125ml) **heavy (double) cream** and pour the mixture into an ice cube tray. When it's frozen, spoon several cubes out into one big refreshing cup.

WARM BANANA TOFFEE MILLE-FEUILLE

This is one of those desserts (or "puddings") that Brits love. They love the super sweet and creamy—like that weird Eton Mess. This one always wins accolades, so why stop a good thing?

Cut a long strip of **puff pastry** (about 10 by 2 inches) and roll it out so it's about ⅛ inch thick. Place it on a baking sheet, cover with another baking sheet or a baking rack (I like the baked-in/deep-line look), and bake at 400°F (200°C) for 10 minutes. Remove the top sheet, sieve **confectioners' sugar (icing sugar)** on top, and return to the oven till crispy and golden brown—a minute or two. Watch closely. Set aside to cool.

Whisk half a cup **mascarpone** with a small spoonful confectioners' sugar and half a scraped **vanilla bean** till fluffy. Set aside.

In a saucepan, combine 3 tablespoons **butter**, ⅓ cup (80ml) **cream or milk**, ¾ cup (150g) **dark brown sugar**, and a tablespoon water. Bring to a boil and simmer until thick and smooth. Let the toffee sauce cool slightly before adding a **banana** (otherwise it will turn to mush), thinly sliced and cut on a diagonal. Keep warm.

Cut the pastry into three equal pieces and trim them into equal-size rectangles. Place one rectangle on a large plate. Spoon or pipe on three small spoons of mascarpone. Gently spoon over a small heap of the bananas in warm toffee sauce. They'll slide down a bit. This is an oozy, messy dish. Repeat with the next layer. Before placing the last rectangle on top, sieve a light dusting of confectioners' sugar on top of it. Now place it on top.

APPLE TURNOVER

Inspired by the apple turnovers at Mickey D's but with ninety-nine fewer ingredients. How 'bout them apples?

FREE-FORM PASTRY

In a bowl, combine half a cup plus 2 tablespoons (90g) **flour**, half a tablespoon **sugar**, a pinch of **salt**, and half a **vanilla bean**, scraped. (You can also add a tablespoon of finely ground **nuts**, if you'd like.) Add 4 tablespoons (60g) cold **butter** and rub the mixture between your hands until crumbly. Drizzle on a little ice cold water just until it comes together. Form into a ball, flatten, wrap in plastic, and let rest in the fridge for at least half an hour.

FILLING

Peel and chop two medium **apples** into small dice. Melt 1 or 2 tablespoons **butter** in a pan, add the apples, a tiny squeeze of **lemon juice**, half a vanilla bean, scraped, a dash of the **booze** of your choice (Calvados, Poire William, Cointreau, whatever), a tablespoon of **sugar or honey**, and a dash of ground **cinnamon**. If the apples are not releasing any liquid (it'll depend on the type), add a few tablespoons water. Cook down gently until they're soft and most of the liquid has been absorbed. Set aside to cool.

Roll out the dough and cut into a circle roughly 8 inches in diameter. Place the circle of dough on a lightly buttered baking sheet. Heap the cooled apple filling onto one side of the circle, leaving a nice edge. It may seem puffy, but the apples will continue to cook down a bit. Besides, a flat turnover looks sad. Moisten the apple edge lightly with water and fold the other half of the dough over the filling. Trim the dough within half an inch of the filling. Prick the edges with the tines of a fork to seal shut. Brush with melted butter. Using the tip of a knife, slash a few half-inch steam vents in the top of the pastry into a pretty, decorative pattern such as a little daisy, a smiley face, or a skull. Bake at 375°F (190°C) until the pastry is golden brown and the apple juices begin to ooze from the vents and trickle down, about 15 to 20 minutes.

"THERE-IS-NO-WAY-IN-HELL-I-AM-WAITING-IN-LINE-FOR-TWO-HOURS" CUPCAKES

We love Manhattan's Magnolia Bakery, but don't you have anything better to do with your time?

In a large bowl, beat 4 tablespoons (60g) soft **butter** with a wooden spoon till it's creamy. Add half a cup (100g) **sugar** and beat till fluffy. Beat in a medium **egg**. Add 6 tablespoons (54g) **self-raising (self-rising) flour**, 5 tablespoons (45g) **plain flour**, a quarter cup (60ml) **light (single) cream**, and a hefty dash of **vanilla extract**. Whisk till smooth.

Spoon into a paper-lined muffin tray. You should have three massive ones or four normal size—either way, a perfect serving. Bake in a 350°F (180°C) oven until light brown and slightly domed—about 20 to 25 minutes. When cool, spoon on a big luscious dollop of . . .

FROSTING

And again with the **butter**: Beat 4 tablespoons till it's creamy. Add 2 cups sifted **confectioners' sugar (icing sugar)** along with just enough **milk** so it's thick and holds a stiff peak (about 2 tablespoons) and finally another dash of **vanilla**. Add a few drops of your favorite food coloring. I like pink.

PIGNOLI BISCOTTI

(Pinoli in Italian. Say it with some gusto.) Lasts forever in an airtight mason jar. Definitely worth doubling.

Toast ⅓ cup (50g) **pignoli nuts** in frying pan. Set aside to cool. Beat 4 tablespoons (60g) very soft **butter** till really creamy. Mix in ⅓ cup (75g) **sugar**, then an **egg**. Scrape in the zest from half a small **lemon** (unwaxed, of course), then squeeze in its **juice**. Add one cup plus one tablespoon **flour** (150g), ¾ teaspoon of **baking powder**, and a tiny pinch of **salt**. Mix well. Stir in the nuts.

Turn out onto a very lightly floured counter and shape into a log about a foot long and one or two inches high. Place on a buttered and floured baking sheet and bake at 325°F (170°C) for about 30 minutes, till lightly browned. Set aside to cool, but keep the oven on.

Slice the biscotti loaf on the diagonal with a serrated knife (you'll get about twelve), place the slices back on the baking sheet, and bake for another 5 to 10 minutes, then flip them over and brown slightly. You want them crisp, dry, and prepped for dunking into a glass of **Passito di Pantelleria**, a dried grape wine from the island of Pantelleria, south of Sicily. The legend of this sweet wine is that the goddess Tanit offered the Greek god Apollo a cup of this magic and he immediately fell in love with her. Things were so uncomplicated then.

BUTTERSCOTCH PANNA COTTA WITH ROASTED MACADAMIA NUT PRALINE

Something I concocted while working at a gastropub in Primrose Hill, London. Remember: a perfect panna cotta should be wobbly and soft, like a woman's (real) breast. The ones with too much silicone, I mean gelatin, don't move. You see it all the time—they just stick straight out, I mean, straight up. Shake the plate back and forth a few times and you'll know right away.

Using a mortar and pestle, very gently crush a handful or two of **butterscotch candies** (any kind in a little wrapper) until they fill up half a cup (115g). Place in a saucepan together with half a scraped **vanilla bean** and ¾ cup (200ml) **light (single) cream.** Cook over low heat, stirring until the candies have melted. Whisk in two leaves of softened **gelatin** until dissolved. Remove from the heat. Add another ¾ cup (200 ml) light cream, whisk, strain, cool, and pour into small molds or ramekins (two to four, depending on size). Chill for a few hours until set.

To remove, fill a small bowl with an inch of hot water and place the mold in it for several seconds until it loosens slightly. Flip over onto a plate, tap it gently, and lift the mold off. Now give it the test.

So, you'll have a few extra, what the hell. Give them to your neighbor. Great alongside a hunk of:

SALTY MACADAMIA NUT PRALINE

Line a small baking sheet with parchment and oil lightly. I'm not big into aerosol vegetable sprays.

In a medium heavy-bottomed stainless steel pan (nonstick=poor results), bring half a cup (100g) **caster sugar** and a quarter cup water to a boil. Let boil slowly until the pace of the bubbles begins to slow down. Here's how you tell it's at the right temperature: take a large slotted spoon, skim through, hold out in front of you, bend down, and blow. If a few big bubbles or one large continuous bubble comes through, you're there (think Mr. Bubbles). If not, let it cook longer. Also, if you have a pastry brush handy (or a brand-new paintbrush), dip it into cold water and wash down the sides of the pan continuously.

Add ¾ cup (100g) roasted **macadamia nuts** (or whatever nut strikes your fancy). Lower the heat slightly. Using a wooden spoon, keep stirring until it all starts to clump together and look sandy. The sugar will then begin to re-melt and slowly caramelize and turn golden. Continue stirring, watching very carefully so the mixture doesn't burn.

Add a small spoonful of unsalted **butter**, quickly stirring until melted. The nuts should be golden and glossy looking. Immediately turn out onto the baking sheet and spread out. Immerse the pan in very hot soapy water *now*.

When the praline is cool, break it up into shards and lightly sprinkle with crushed **Maldon salt**, if desired.

Keep what's left in an airtight container or give it to your neighbor.

WILD BLUEBERRY TART

The chances of finding these tiny wild blueberries even in sea-son are pretty slim, but I thought the name sounded inviting. If you can source them, do know that this superfruit is ridicu-lously good for you. I mean, off the charts. But the big, fat burst-ing ones are also great. This little tart is free form in shape—so again, no equipment or fancy tart rings required.

Make the **free-form pastry dough** from the Apple Turnover recipe on page 168. Wrap it up and let chill in the fridge.

In a small saucepan, stir together a pint of washed **blueberries** (or other fresh berries), a spoonful each of **sugar** and **cornstarch**, and a squeeze of **lemon juice**. You can also add a dash of **Cointreau**. Gently simmer until it starts to become really thick. Remove from the heat and scoop into a small bowl.

Wash out the saucepan. Add an **egg**, **egg yolk**, 2 teaspoons of **sugar**, and the same amount of freshly squeezed **lemon juice**. Whisk directly and rapidly over *low* heat. You can do this over a bain-marie to ensure perfection, but I say go for it. Whisk rapidly, being careful not to let it curdle and turn into scrambled eggs. It'll be quick—there's not a lot. When your *sabayon* begins to thicken, add a teaspoon or two of **butter** and continue whisking. Add a tablespoon of **light (single) cream** and remove from the heat. The sabayon should be thick and luscious. If you do find any lumps, don't look at them. Or, just press the mixture through a sieve using a rubber spatula. Set aside.

Okay, last part. Take out your dough, cut in two, and freeze half. Work the other half with your hands until it softens slightly. Place on a lightly floured sheet of parchment, and using a rolling pin (or your hands), pat down into a ⅛-inch circle. It's rustic, remember, not delicate. Trim the edges with a knife, and keeping the parchment underneath, place on a baking sheet. Spoon the sabayon onto the bottom of the dough, leaving a 1- to 1½-inch border, then spoon on the blueberries, so it's heaping. Now to finish up: we're going for a tulip-shaped tart—only squashed. Fold over five edges inward, one "petal" at a time, hiding the filling slightly. That's about it. Bake at 350°F (180°C) until brown and bubbly—about 15 minutes. Serve with vanilla ice cream. Whipped cream takes too long to make.

Ideally, this tart should be slipped onto a stone base and baked like pizza, but you can't always get what you want. Also, you can skip the sabayon and just layer in sliced fruit—from peaches to plums in the summer and pears to kumquats in the winter. Sprinkle with small cubes of butter, then with sugar or a drizzle of wild honey (chestnut honey is lovely here), and bake till the fruit is soft and the pastry is golden.

AFFOGATO

I've seen this on dessert menus for ten dollars, ten pounds, and ten euros. Insanity. But of course the ice cream is imported from a fourteenth-century monastery deep in the hills of Siena, where a group of nuns hand-squeeze the milk from baby cows that are fed an exclusive diet of hand-picked organic wheatgrass and chestnut honey from their local bee farms (they are very happy cows). Then the anglaise is prepared and bottled by the nuns themselves into recycled glass jugs and transported via the Tyrrhenian Sea by their one and only dinghy boat. Also bear in mind that each espresso bean is hand-roasted with tender loving care by the local farmers in nearby Montopoli Val d'Arno, or one of those places. They work only three hours a week (they're Italian), so it takes a really long time.

I'd be the sucker and order it anyway.

Make an **espresso** or cup of **coffee**. Pour into a glass. Plop in a scoop of your favorite **ice cream**. Spoon into your mouth.

AN HOMAGE TO WILLY WONKA

Those who use chocolate ordinarily enjoy the most perfect health, and are the least subject to the multitude of ailments which destroy life.

—BRILLAT-SAVARIN

I find it slightly disturbing when a person claims they "don't really like chocolate." *Are you freaking kidding me?* Serious issues. Control freaks, usually. I am quite proud of the fact that I've eaten chocolate in some way, shape, or percentage of cocoa solids almost every single day of my sweet life. I mean, pour molten chocolate over Willy Wonka himself, and I will gladly lap it off him and savor every last delectable lick (assuming it's the Johnny Depp version and not the Gene Wilder one).

It began at about age five. Our weekly grocery shopping trips to the A&P were the highlight of my week, particularly the checkout part. This consisted of my mother sorting through a foot-high pile of coupons, the cashier glaring on, and my sisters in the grocery cart battling it out in their version of *American Idol.* My younger sister, Michelle, would be in the front basket crooning "Over the Rainbow" with an incredibly long ribbon dangling down each side of her head. This was her attempt at creating pigtails like Dorothy's. My older sister, Leonora, would be in the back singing "My Country 'Tis of Thee" or something equally disturbing. But they served as ample distraction for my mission.

I'd be at the candy bar section behind them. How savvy to have designed it at (my) eye level. I would carefully deliberate over the Snickers, Almond Joy, or Reese's Peanut Butter Cups double pack, and choose only one (I wasn't greedy). Then I'd stick it down my pants and walk very slowly with the three of them out the door. When we returned home, I'd make a beeline into my bedroom closet, nestle into my spot, and snarf it down.

My new devil-may-care attitude piqued my mother's curiosity. Finally, I was caught in the act. As I sat squatting behind the piles of mothball boxes with my Snickers bar, she slid the closet door open.

"I am very disappointed in you," my mother said as she shook her head sternly. Those words were the worst.

I was immediately confined to my bedroom for the day. As I lay on my twin bed plotting how I'd manage to get my next fix, I noticed my sister's plastic Halloween pumpkin poking out from under her bed. It was filled to the brim with miniature Hershey bars. I had no idea she was such a stingy minger. My only question was, how would I discard the evidence? I decided that I would discreetly climb behind our living room couch, cram a Hershey bar in my mouth, and simply leave the wrapper behind. No one ever went back there.

My secret daily fix went well over the next month, until my mother decided to vacuum. As she pulled the couch out in one fell swoop, all the Hershey wrappers leapt out and danced around in schadenfreude. Bastards. She shot me a look. A look and a dagger. I nonchalantly shrugged my shoulders and suggested it was the carnage from some crazed vermin infestation. And just at that moment, my sister, Dorothy, in full drama queen mode, ran downstairs screaming. She held her near-empty Halloween pumpkin up into the air, as crocodile tears streamed down her face. She was such a whiner. My mother shook her head sternly and said, "I am *very* disappointed in you." She was killing me.

Two weeks later, as I stood on a chair, freezer door open, devouring a gallon of chocolate chocolate-chip fudge swirl ice cream (I think it was Breyer's or something), my father caught me red-handed. Only this time, I got a wicked spanking.

As you know, if something pleasurable is denied, it becomes an obsession. And I've made it a point to never deny myself anything pleasurable. Obsessions are for wimps.

Recently on a trip to Thailand, I became engrossed in a conversation with a raw food expert named Francis. As we sipped the cacahuatis he made using raw cocoa beans, almond milk, honey, vanilla, and chiles (an acquired taste, though certainly not a Coffee Bean Ultimate Ice Blended, which truly is the ultimate), he recounted the litany of reasons I must surrender to the life-changing benefits of a raw food diet. But instead, I became completely transfixed by his physical appearance. His crickety bones protruded at every conceivable angle. I knew I could easily knock him out with one punch.

Francis said that only raw cocoa beans, as opposed to roasted, had magical powers. I knew I had to stop him there. First of all, he obviously hadn't seen the movie *Chocolat*. Juliette Binoche single-handedly transformed an entire town of repressed and angry zealots into wild and lusty animals because and only because of her magical chocolate confections. In one scene, even the lovely Ms. Binoche couldn't stop herself from lapping up molten chocolate from her naked lover, played by Johnny Depp. But that scene was cut.

Francis was a fascinating character, but I'm a hard sell. Regardless of one's preference over raw or roasted, I'm certainly never thinking about how theobroma ("food of the gods") has psychotropic properties containing theobromine, methylxanthine, and phenylethylalanine, which act as stimulants to my dopamine and adrenaline levels and tell my brain to release endorphins and simulate that euphoric feeling of being in love (mmh) . . . or that the flavanols in the cocoa beans of my minimally processed 70 percent dark chocolate have an antioxidant potency four times greater than that of green tea, which blocks arterial damage caused by millions of those free radicals . . . yada yada.

You see, all I want is some fucking chocolate. Now.

No sharing, and nothing raw.

WARM CHOCOLATE FONDANT

I think you'll be delighted with this.

In a small saucepan over very low heat, melt half a cup (90g) of your very best **70 percent chocolate**, finely chopped. You need to be careful that it doesn't begin to cook, so here's what you do: As soon as a little chocolate begins to melt, remove the pan from the heat and begin stirring it with a rubber spatula. Return to the heat again just briefly for a few seconds, stirring continuously, then take off the heat again, stirring. Repeat this one or two more times, as necessary, until the chocolate is completely melted. This really only takes about four minutes in total. Set aside.

In a bowl, cream together one tablespoon (15g) very soft **butter** and ¼ cup (30g) unsifted **confectioners' sugar (icing sugar)** (the mixture will be crumbly, don't worry), then a medium **egg**, and whisk until it's completely smooth. Stir in the melted chocolate. Lastly, add one tablespoon (9g) **flour** and a tiny sprinkling of **sea salt** and mix well.

Lightly butter one mold (ramekin, dariole, you know the deal), and if you have some **unsweetened cocoa**, dust a little in and tap out the excess. Spoon in the batter and bake at 400°F (200°C) for 9 to 11 minutes. It should look like a baby Mount Etna (use Google Image if you have to). If you cook it for too long, even a minute, it'll become chocolate cake and that's not the recipe, dammit. Your molten lava will be cooked. Flip over onto a large plate and unmold the fondant. Serve with a decent scoop of **vanilla ice cream** alongside.

A wine paired with a dessert needs to be richer and sweeter than the dessert itself. In this case, the fondant will not send you into a sugar coma. Suggested pairing here: **Barolo Chinato**, Cappellano NV.

PEANUT BUTTER CUPS

Way better than Reese's, even without the ten-syllable ingredients.

With a wooden spoon, beat ¼ cup (60g) smooth all-natural **peanut butter,** one teaspoon of very soft **butter,** and ¼ cup (28g) sifted **confectioners' sugar (icing sugar)** until smooth. Transfer into a sturdy quart size plastic bag (your makeshift pastry bag) and set aside.

Melt half a cup (100g) **dark 70 percent chocolate** using the instructions from the Chocolate Fondant, page 181. Or melt in a double boiler. Dip the back of a spoon in and use the melted chocolate to coat the insides of several very tiny paper cup liners (see Sources, page 217). Not too thin, or the chocolate will crack when you peel the paper off. Place on a plate and into the freezer to set—10 to 20 minutes.

Tightly wind one end of the bag around so that the peanut butter filling is firmly in place at the other end. Cut off the tip of one end of the bag. Pipe the filling into the cups until about three-quarters full. Using a small spoon, cover with the remaining melted chocolate. Eat immediately or refrigerate till the top hardens. Pop each in your mouth with a sip of **Lustau Moscatel** "Emilin" NV.

A BROWNIE

I was thinking about that famous Alice B. Toklas brownie rec-
ipe. But I say, why not just roll up a big fat one and smoke it
before you make it? Your enjoyment could be tripled. I just love
my brownie as is—crackly on top, moist and slightly fudgey in
the middle, and never ever sickeningly sweet.

Pile 4 tablespoons (60g) **butter** in a small saucepan and let about
half of it melt slowly, coating the bottom. Then pile ⅓ cup (50g) of
your favorite chopped **70 percent dark chocolate** on top (try artisanal Sampaka chips from Spain—www.cacaosampaka.com—for a
hint of smoky cinnamon). Let melt together over very low heat,
stirring until incorporated. Set aside.

In a medium bowl, whisk one **egg** till pale yellow and frothy.
Then whisk in ⅓ cup plus 1 tablespoon (80g) **sugar**, and a dash of
vanilla, and then the melted butter and chocolate. Stir in 2 tablespoons (18g) **flour** and a tiny pinch of crushed **sea salt**. Lastly, stir
in a large handful of roughly chopped and toasted **walnuts**. A
must.

Pour into a small, lightly buttered mold and bake at 350°F
(180°C). You want a slightly wet center, but not oozy—about 15 to
20 minutes.

Oh, and place your little mold on a baking sheet or you'll wind up with some nasty third-degree burns, your reward for attempting to remove it from your oven in a gluttonous hurry. I know you're desperate, but this is very important.

Those burns suck.

MELT-IN-YOUR-MOUTH CHOCOLATE COOKIES

Cookies for one? That's the stupidest thing I've ever heard of.

Beat a half cup (1 stick) plus 2 tablespoons very soft **butter** (150g). Mix in half a cup **sugar** (100g) and a dash of **vanilla extract**. Stir in one cup plus 5 tablespoons **flour** (195g), 2 tablespoons **unsweetened cocoa** (18g), a pinch of **cinnamon**, and a pinch of **Maldon salt**. It will be dry—this is okay. Pour the dough out onto counter and use the heel of your hand to *fraisage* the dough until it comes together. Pat together into a log about 2 inches in diameter. Roll up in plastic wrap and let chill in the fridge until firm.

The log will make about fifteen cookies, so slice off a chunk of what you'd like to bake. The rest of the log can be wrapped in plastic and frozen for later—just slice 'n' bake. Beat an **egg** with a little water, dip your fingers in, and lightly coat your little chunk all over with egg wash. Of course, if you have a pastry brush, that's also acceptable. Then coat it evenly in **sugar**. Slice the cookies about half an inch thick, place on a baking sheet, and bake at 350°F (180°C) until they're just firm—about 10 minutes. Your finger should make a slight imprint when you lightly press on one. If you bake them for too long, they'll be like rocks and we'll have to change the name. Let cool.

Dunk your cookies into a glass of 2004 **Vin Santo del Chianti Classico** from Isole e Olena.

VALRHONA CHOCOLATE TRUFFLES

I have enormous respect for the chocolatier. In this recipe, using only two ingredients as a base (chocolate and cream), the resulting possibilities are endless. The trick is all in the technique and the minutest of details. But let's not fret already, just begin.

Very finely chop some **Valrhona Caraïbe chocolate** (or any of your best 70 percent chocolate) and measure out half a cup (80g). Place half in a medium bowl with a small dish towel underneath (in case the counter is too cool) and keep the rest of the chocolate in a small bowl close by. Bear with me here, we're dealing with such a small amount that it's easy to mess up in a matter of seconds. I have, many times. Pour ⅓ cup plus 1 tablespoon (100g) **heavy (double) cream** into a saucepan and bring it to a boil. Your next goal here is: work fast/no lumps/keep glossy. Pour *half* the cream over the chocolate in the medium bowl and whisk quickly until it's perfectly smooth. Now return that little bit of cream to the heat and bring it to a boil again till it's bubbling. Quickly whisk the rest of the chocolate to the chocolate/cream mixture (which will be lumpy), then whisk in the remainder of the bubbling cream till the ganache is perfectly smooth and glossy. If it's not, better luck next time.

Let cool and then place in the fridge, covered, until firm—a few hours or overnight.

Line a plate with parchment. Sift a few spoonfuls of **unsweet-ened cocoa powder** (preferably Valrhona Dutch processed) into a bowl. Scoop out a tablespoon of the ganache, shape it into a little ball (don't fuss—it should be somewhat misshapen), drop in, then roll the ball gently into the cocoa. Place the truffle in a small sieve and shake off any extra cocoa so that when you bite into one, you won't inhale the excess and choke. Place on the plate. Repeat with the rest of the ganache. Wrap the plate well and store in the fridge. Makes about six to eight truffles.

VARIATION 1

Try your own combination of chocolates from Mexico, Venezuela, Ecuador, Madagascar, the Caribbean, Australia . . . the different qualities will create interesting results.

VARIATION II

You can infuse the chocolate with ingredients from the list below. Add to the cream before boiling, then seal the saucepan with plastic wrap and infuse for about 10 minutes (or longer for a stronger flavor—taste along the way). After straining the cream over the chocolate, carefully reheat the cream so that it's hot enough to melt the chocolate properly.

The amounts listed are a gentle guideline—experiment with abandon.

Espresso, freshly ground—about 2 teaspoons
Vanilla beans—2 scraped and with pods
Cinnamon—2 or 3 sticks

Nutmeg—several gratings

Fresh ginger, peeled and sliced—about 2 tablespoons

Habañero or ancho chiles, dried and crushed—a teaspoon

Szechuan peppercorns (more sweet than heat) toasted and crushed—a tablespoon

Aniseed—a tablespoon

Fresh mint—half a cup, snipped

Fresh rosemary—half a cup, coarsely chopped

Fresh lavender—half a cup, cut with scissors into 1-inch pieces

Fresh orange—several wide rinds

Fresh lemon (unwaxed, please)—several wide rinds

Earl Grey tea leaves—a quarter cup

Jasmine tea leaves—a quarter cup

Lapsang souchong tea leaves—a quarter cup

I think chamomile would be gross.

VARIATION III

Add to the ganache:

Nuts—any kind, roasted and finely chopped

Feuilletine—similar to crispy tuile cookies, finely crushed

Praline—finely crushed in a mortar and pestle (see Salty Macadamia Nut Praline, page 173)

Coconut—either kind, the crunchy desiccated or the moist and flaky

Nutella—a spoonful

Chopped Snickers bar . . . caramels . . . candied oranges . . .

Booze such as whisky and rum (a small glug)

Liqueurs such as Grand Marnier, Cointreau, Cassis, Frangelico . . .

Shall I continue?

Serve with a glass of **Banyuls Cuvée de la St. Martin**, Domaine du Mas Blanc 1979, of course.

CHOCOLATE ICE CREAM FLOAT

A great after-school pick-me-up for you and the kids.

Bring ¼ cup **sugar**, 2 tablespoons **Valrhona cocoa powder**, and 3 tablespoons water to a boil and simmer till thickened. Let cool.

Put a few big scoops of **chocolate ice cream** in one of those tall, ridged ice cream parlor–type glasses. Pour the chocolate syrup on top, then a shot of **Jack Daniel's** or dark rum, and fill the glass with chilled **club soda**. You'll need a straw. Give a stir and suck it down.

BREAD AND CHOCOLATE

Toast a thin slice of **Poilâne** or any thinly sliced rustic bread. Place on a plate. Top with a slab of your favorite **dark chocolate** the same thickness as the bread. Drizzle with an excellent **extra virgin olive oil**. Sift a little **unsweetened cocoa** across in one sweep. Sprinkle with crushed **fleur de sel**. Eat with a knife and fork.

MÉNAGE À DEUX

The forms of virtue are direct; the forms of pleasure, undulate.

——HENRY FUSELI

He offered to cook. I accepted. I soon learned that his offer had no hidden agenda. It was pure economics—budget for dinner: $4.63. For two. And, he had to eat. He was a supermodel who had just been dumped by Claudia Schiffer. She left him their Murray Hill duplex town house, the bed, and a baby grand. The rest remained empty except for a bowl of hotel soaps in the master bathroom. Those were his.

The dinner went something like this: two chicken breasts, out of package, into pan. One slice of Kraft American cheese placed on top of each breast, into oven, and left in there for a really long time. He was pretty smart—if you cook the shit out of something, you won't get salmonella. Plum tomatoes, out of tin, placed around plate. Wine was not in the budget. He insisted we sit on the kitchen counters to eat. He did have two forks, which was nice. The veins in the chicken were a bit tricky to cut without a knife, but did give it a chewy texture. It was edible in a *Ready Steady Cook* kind of way. Was this meal the last straw for Claudia?

But come on, I thought, it's never really about *what* you cook, but rather about the effort inv . . . oh . . . wait, hold on . . .

He offered to cook. I accepted. I soon learned that his offer had a hidden agenda. He really wanted to impress me. He was the older, erudite British man educating the naïve and newly relocated American woman in classic British fare. He was so smart that I barely minded his clackety lockjaw when we kissed. He decided he'd cook me a Sunday roast—my very first.

I eagerly anticipated an eye-opening culinary adventure: Bedfordshire Clanger . . . Pan Haggerty . . . Singin Hinnies . . . whatever they looked like. Anyway, upon entering his flat (with an incredibly expensive bottle of wine to exonerate myself for being late but impressively hungover), I was immediately blasted with the overwhelming smell of vinegar. He seemed to have just washed his windows. He certainly went all out. Then I started to feel really guilty, so I ate a few of his amuse-bouches: Tesco's sausage rolls. After an enthusiastic three or four, they made me throw up in my mouth a little. He offered me red wine (sadly not mine, which had been quickly shelved), and I forced it down to be polite. We then sat at opposite ends of a rather long and steel black dining table.

The roast went something like this: pork belly (note: if you don't cook the shit out of that lump, the fat is just that: fat), boiled greens, and puréed apples. He spoke of his attempt at making a beurre blanc sauce (hence the vinegar) but I assured him that he had already put himself out far too much. He proudly revealed that the menu was a family tradition passed down from many generations of his remarkably regal family and was prepared while on the phone with his mum. I don't know, the Oedipus thing is endearing until about . . . eight? Okay, nine, max. After that, it's just creepy. I'll skip the part about his flatmates. Only that having them when you're over forty-five is a deal-breaker.

So I gave him one last kiss, he gave me one last clack, and I cabbed it home to the unsurpassed comfort of my bed, which was still warm.

He offered to cook. I accepted. I soon learned that his offer had a serious agenda, and there would be no holds barred. He was my neighbor, he was hot, and I liked him. As I began my journey up four flights of stairs to his flat, I became slowly bewitched by an increasing potency of aromas and sounds. First came the violins of a Puccini aria and the hint of wood-roasted garlic. The next flight was sweet simmering roasted tomatoes and the faint yet fragrant hint of roasting meats. A few more steps up and Puccini unveiled himself to "Ancora un paso or via," Madama Butterfly's entrance. It was stupidly perfect.

When I reached the fourth floor, he greeted me outside the door. He handed me a short tumbler and poured from a chilled bottle of Txakoli, three feet high above the glass. It came down fast, in a steady stream, fizzling bubbles dancing in the glass. He spilled a bit, but it was cute. I smiled, and said that a Basquian feast would be impressive. He said it was his favorite aperitif and just liked the taste of it.

We strolled inside and nibbled on a few bruschetta with a

garlicky black olive tapenade. He then disappeared into his un-adorned man-kitchen. He returned shortly with two plates piled high with steamy linguine bathed in an unfussy thyme-infused roasted tomato sauce of hand-cut veal, pork, and beef with jagged shards of pecorino and cracked black pepper. He sat down next to me on a Spartan wooden bench behind a rustic dark walnut farm table overlooking . . . well, the view wasn't great. Anyway, he gently leaned over and kissed the nape of my neck with guileless spontane-ity. The exquisite bottle of red was a '98 Ornellaia—luscious and black cherried, from Antinori. Liquid candy.

For a moment I thought, he didn't seem gay. Or even remotely metrosexual, except for the three or four unnecessary bottles of Kiehl's products lined up on his bathroom shelf. He just had good training somewhere down the line. I just went with it. Dessert was tiramisù, but we never got there.

On my way out the next morning, I peeked into his kitchen to admire the mess I wouldn't have to clean, but was impressed to find only a ridiculous overflow of garbage spilling out of the bin. I gently opened the lid to give it all a quick push. The take-away trays were still intact. He was so smart. And I was very happy.

BONUS RECIPES

For when you're stuck with large quantities of ingredients.

DUCK CONFIT, PAGE 17

DUCK RAGU WITH PAPPARADELLE

Sweat mirepoix: a tablespoon each of diced **carrot** and **celery** and 2 tablespoons **onion** in **olive oil** till soft. Add a few tablespoons of **Vin Santo** and stir in a few large skinned and seeded **tomatoes**, one **duck leg confit** (skinned and shredded), a pinch of **hot red chili powder**, and a small pinch of **ground cloves**. Simmer gently until the tomatoes are soft. Season with **Maldon salt** and a little **sugar**, if desired. Toss in a few handfuls of cooked **pappardelle** and heat through.

DUCK RILLETTE

Wipe off the fat from a **duck leg**. Remove the skin and shred the meat well into a bowl. Using a mortar and pestle, grind down a little minced **shallot**, **garlic** (or garlic confit), and a little coarsely chopped **fresh flat-leaf parsley**. Add the mixture to the shredded duck along with a teaspoon of **cognac**. Add in enough **duck fat** so the mixture comes together (1 to 3 tablespoons). Season with **black pepper**. Serve with delicate toasted French bread slices or hunks of toasted peasant bread . . . or store in a sterilized mason jar (wash it in hot soapy water and dry in the oven at low heat for 15 minutes). Lasts for a few weeks.

FOIE GRAS, PAGE 70

- **Stuffing**

  Have your butcher bone the cavity of a **squab** or other small bird. Sweat one tablespoon of a finely chopped **shallot** in **olive oil**. Lower the heat and stir in a spoonful of **currants**. Deglaze with a dash of **armagnac** or **port** so that the currants become soft and drunken. Add a cup of cubed fresh **bread** (small dice) and chopped **fresh thyme**. Add **chicken stock** to moisten. Mix 2 tablespoons cubed fresh **foie gras** into the stuffing and season to taste. Stuff the bird. Seal the cavity with toothpicks and roast at 425°F (220°C) for 20 to 30 minutes, until the juices run slightly pink when you prick with a fork in the thickest part of the leg. Rest before serving.

- See the Elena Arzak recipe for Clips de Cogollos con Mango, page 80.

- Think Daniel Boulud, chef extraordinaire, and his burger at DB Moderne: take a large cube of fresh **foie gras** and stuff it inside your Big Ol' Burger (see page 134). Pan-fry the burger accordingly.

BACALAO (SALT COD)

BAKED SALT COD FILLET

In *The Art of Eating Well*, published in 1891, Pellegrino Artusi claims that salt cod should never be fried—and anyone who fries it will be damned to hell. What a silly little man.

Cut off a portion (fillet-size) of your hefty piece of **salt cod**. Rinse it well, place it in a bowl, and cover it—a few inches above—with cold water. Keep in the fridge overnight up to 24 hours, rinsing it at least four times. That's the magic number here. When you're ready to eat it, dry really well, sprinkle each side with **white pepper**, and pan-sear in hot **olive oil** a few minutes on each side till golden. Remove and place in small casserole dish or cazuela. In the same pan and with a bit more oil, add a minced **garlic clove** (the pan will still be damn hot, so keep it off the heat until the garlic gets some color). Deglaze with a nice glug of **dry sherry** and a dash of **pimentón de La Vera**. Return to the heat and let reduce till slightly thickened—it will be a rich brown color. Stir in a little finely chopped **fresh flat-leaf parsley**, season to taste, pour over the cod, and bake at around 350°F (180°C) for 5 to 10 minutes, till piping hot.

BACALAO WITH FRESH ORANGE AND BLACK OLIVES

Prep a fillet of **salt cod** as above. Drain well, dry well, and shred, discarding every last bone. Slice the skin from a fresh **orange** or sweet pink grapefruit (pith removed and sliced in half with stems on each side—you'll only need half). Slice the orange into thin rounds and place in a single layer on a plate. Sprinkle with a touch of **sea salt**. Scatter on the shredded salt cod. Slice a small **Spanish** or

red onion incredibly thin and place several slices on top. Hastily chop some black **Spanish olives**. Drizzle on a few drops of a decent **sherry vinegar** or squeeze of **lemon** followed with a drizzle of an excellent **extra virgin olive oil**. A little crushed **black pepper** and perhaps some roughly chopped **fresh parsley** if you have some, and you're good to go. There are usually chopped green peppers in this classic, but I hate them, so they're out.

BAKED POTATOES, PAGE 13

GNOCCHI

Press the *hot* filling from two baked potatoes through a sieve. Add half a cup **flour** and pinch of **Maldon salt**. Add about half a beaten **egg** until the mixture softens and is like dough. Turn out onto floured counter and knead slightly until soft and dry.

Roll into a long rope about half an inch thick. Slice the dough into one-inch pieces. Drop into gently simmering and salted water until they just float—it'll be quick. Toss into brown **butter**, grated **parmigiano**, and cracked **black pepper**—or into the Duck Ragu or with the Guanciale e Prezzemolo in this section.

DUCK FAT, PAGE 17

Use for pan-roasted **vegetables** (think Alain Ducasse), or to deep-fry your **fries**, or in **hash browns**: Into a frying pan with hot melted duck fat, coarsely shred a potato in a single layer. Season well. Let cook until brown, flip, and fry the other side. Drain and top with a poached egg.

LEMONGRASS

MUSSELS IN LEMONGRASS BROTH

Bash up a few **lemongrass** stalks to crush them and release their elegant fragrance (a hammer works), cut them into 2-inch pieces (no smaller because they'll shred and you'll be pulling them out of your teeth), and throw them in a medium pot with 1½ to 2 cups of **dashi** (Japanese stock) and a small thinly sliced **red chile pepper**. Mix about 2 tablespoons of **fish sauce** together with an equal amount of freshly squeezed **lime juice**, then half that of **palm sugar**. Add to the stock, bring to a boil, and reduce it all down slightly till the aromas are outstanding. Now add lots of fresh **mussels** that have been scrubbed and de-bearded (I go for about four to five handfuls or one pound (500g) for an entrée portion). Cover with a lid and cook the mussels until they have popped open—just a few minutes. Serve them in a large bowl with the soup ladled over and coarsely chopped **fresh basil** and/or **cilantro** on top. Nice with a bowl of jasmine rice: Rinse half a cup **jasmine rice** and add to one cup of water and a pinch of **sea salt**. Bring to a boil, cover, and let simmer till cooked and fluffy—about 20 minutes.

STEAMED FISH

Cut out a large circle of parchment paper and place a fillet of **sea bass** on one side. Sprinkle each side lightly with **sea salt** and **white**

pepper. Sprinkle on a sliced **red chile pepper**, two julienned **kaffir lime leaves**, and a bashed stalk of **lemongrass**, cut into 1- or 2-inch pieces. Fold over and crimp securely or staple together, leaving a small vent for steam to escape. Place in a shallow baking dish. Pour in enough **white wine or fish stock** through the vent to cover the fish so it'll poach nicely. Bake in 400°F (200°C) oven for about 15 to 20 minutes. Open carefully—no steam burns, please. Serve with rice.

GUANCIALE

PASTA CON GUANCIALE E PREZZEMOLO
(Pasta with Cured Pig Cheeks and Parsley)

My favorite. Cook a portion of your favorite type of **pasta** (I prefer bucatini, although I'll use anything from penne to orecchiette) and reserve a cup of pasta water. Fry very thinly sliced **guanciale** in a little **olive oil** with a good pinch of crushed dried **chile flakes**. Remove from the pan and set aside. In the same oil, and over low heat, sweat a few minced **garlic cloves**, then deglaze with half a cup reserved pasta water. As soon as it starts to boil, add a spoonful of **butter**, lots of finely grated **parmigiano or pecorino**, and the guanciale to make the sauce. Stir in the pasta and a bit more pasta water, if necessary. Finish with chopped **fresh flat-leaf parsley** and **cracked black pepper** (and a pinch **Maldon salt**, if needed). Pour into a bowl and top with paper-thin slices of parmigiano or pecorino.

SCRAPS OF PASTA DOUGH, PAGE 61

SCIALATIELLI CON POMODORI CILIEGE ARROSTI
(Homemade Flat Pasta with Roasted Cherry Tomatoes)

I know, I know, but I just can't stop myself with all the Italian, which I don't really speak a word of, but it's so frigging sexy. In 300°F (150°C) oven, slowly roast a pint of **cherry tomatoes** in season in a small tray with a good drizzle of **olive oil**, a dash of **white balsamic vinegar**, a few unpeeled **garlic cloves**, **Maldon salt**, **cracked black pepper**, and a pinch of **red chile flakes**. Let the tomatoes roast till they pop and start to break down lightly—about 20 to 30 minutes. Squeeze out the garlic from the skins and mix lightly into the sauce. Toss over cooked **scialatielli** (will only take 2 to 3 minutes to cook) and mix in torn **fresh basil leaves**. Garnish with any of the usual suspects (**parmigiano**, **pecorino**, **grana padano**, or for something different, dollops of fresh **ricotta**). Drizzle with a little more olive oil.

SEVEN USES FOR EXTRA MASCARPONE OR CRÈME FRAÎCHE

1) Mix with a few glugs of **olive oil** and smashed **garlic** cloves and use to marinate poultry; 2) add a spoonful at the end of a simple **pasta** dish—perhaps one made with **lemon zest, garlic, chives**, and **parsley**; 3) mix into **tomato sauce** just before tossing with **pasta**;

4) spoon in at the end of a **wild mushroom** or **saffron risotto**; 5) add a spoonful at the end of the **Home-Style Yellow Split Peas** on page 36—it'll transform into a creamy risotto; 6) whisk into **scrambled eggs** while they're cooking; 7) for a snack, mix with a creamy and tangy cheese, such as **Roquefort**, and some chopped **herbs**, then spoon onto a thick slice of **toast**. Top with a handful of **watercress** or arugula.

HERBS

PISTOU/PESTO

Pistou (traditionally with basil, but try with cilantro or all that flat-leaf parsley): Mash a **garlic clove** in a mortar and pestle and pound in a cup or more of stemmed and roughly chopped **herbs**. Add enough **olive oil** to make a sauce. Season with **Maldon salt** and **pepper**. Add a dollop to a bowl of the **Classic Winter Vegetable Soup** on page 122, or spoon on a fresh and oozy burrata mozzarella (or any cheese of your choice, although I wouldn't recommend blue) and sliced seasonal tomatoes—for a **bruschetta**.

If you add ground roasted nuts such as pignoli, walnuts, or pistachios to the pistou, it becomes a lovely **pesto**. Store in an airtight container with a thin layer of olive oil on top. Go crazy. Have a party.

SALSA VERDE

This seems innocent enough, but the taste is absolutely fierce. I love it. In mortar and pestle, grind down one peeled and smashed **garlic clove**. Add an **anchovy** or two, four or five **capers**, and a squeeze of fresh **lemon juice**. Coarsely chop the leaves (no stems here) of a cup each of **fresh basil** and **flat-leaf parsley**, adding enough **olive oil** till it's thick (about half a cup). Add a small dash of **sherry wine vinegar** (or red wine vinegar) and season to taste with **cracked black pepper**. Serve alongside grilled lamb, steak, chicken, or a meaty white fish; grilled, roasted, or steamed vegetables; or stir into any cooked pasta.

SALAD

Use whole leaves of herbs in various combinations to liven up any green salad.

For example, add basil, mint, and cilantro to a crunchy or stronger tasting green such as romaine, arugula, spinach. Add the more delicate herbs such as flat-leaf parsley, chives, tarragon, chervil to more delicate and soft greens such as mâche or Boston lettuce.

A MOJITO

For extra mint, make yourself a mojito. I learned how to bartend, properly, from a true craftsman—an artisan, really. The pride and passion that went into every single one of his cocktails was quite extraordinary. For one, he created the Cosmopolitan, ubiquitous now, pioneering then. (And I don't care what anyone tries to tell you, he was the one.) I was awe-inspired (but never told him that, of course) as we worked together behind the bar at Kin Khao on Thompson Street in Manhattan. He turned a simple cocktail into an art form. I'd like to dedicate one of my favorite cocktails to him (although he'd probably spit it out—he was a perfectionist, let me tell you). We'll call it:

THE TOBY CECCHINI

Dissolve a heaping tablespoon of **sugar** in a little hot water. Pour into a tall, chilled highball glass. Add about half a cup *snipped* **fresh mint leaves** (love, baby, bring on the love) and muddle them around with a pair of chopsticks or something. Carefully crack a lot of **ice** (not too small) using a mortar and pestle to give it a stylish 1920s-lounging-in-your-cabana-by-the-pool look. Spoon the ice into the glass. Now pour in your twenty-three-year-old Ron Zacapa Centenario **rum** (see Cake, page 164)—a few shots should do it. Squeeze in the juice from a whole fresh **lime**, which has been kneaded and warmed in your hands. Stir. As for the mint garnish—as I said before, I don't do them. A straw is handy but never necessary. Cheers, Toby!

YOUR BARE-BONES CUPBOARD

Every cookbook out there has an excellent list of staple ingredients. Let's assume you already have them. While shopping, words like local . . . organic . . . free-range . . . wild . . . seasonal . . . dolphin-friendly . . . eco-friendly . . . are all part of your vocabulary. You know your shop owners. They like you.

When cooking for yourself, you have the unique opportunity to try out the highest quality of ingredients, which can either assuage your curiosity ("Wow, I *love* foie gras!") or lambaste certain myths ("Wow, truffles are lame"). And remember, a portion for one certainly costs far less than a portion for six.

The essential ingredients that I (strongly) suggest using are:

SEA SALT. MALDON: Why, you ask? Because it's easy to use—you can crush a pinch of the icy flakes between your fingers; it's mild, has no additives, and no aftertaste. If it's the only thing you add to a dish, it'll still make a huge improvement.

WHOLE BLACK AND WHITE PEPPERCORNS: Crushed in a mortar and pestle or pepper mill just before using each time. Buy the bags at local Asian markets. Much cheaper.

EXTRA VIRGIN OLIVE OIL: Always. You should know better by now.

FRESH STOCKS: Meaning, freshly bought. If you make them yourself, you get a gold star. Can be frozen. Never use stock cubes, I don't care which chef is promoting them. If you're in a bind, have a few of More Than Gourmet's dehydrated stocks on hand (roasted chicken, fish, veal demi-glace, mushroom, reduced brown stocks— they have it all). They're all natural, and nothing weird is added. I use about half of a small container per 2 cups water for a single portion of risotto. Go to www.morethangourmet.com.

CHESTNUT HONEY: Indulgent but necessary. Use it instead of regular honey—drizzled over a hunk of pecorino for dessert is the best. Classic.

EXCELLENT 70 PERCENT DARK CHOCOLATE: I am partial to Valrhona when baking. The results are always consistent.

IN THE FRIDGE AT ALL TIMES

BREAD: Anything without unnatural ingredients. The good ones have four: flour, sea salt, water, and a rising agent (not necessarily yeast). The flour is stone-ground wheat, the salt is from Guérande, the water is from the Alps, and the rising agent is from a starter using fermented apples (a long artisanal process). And it's baked in a wood-fired oven. Wait, did I say **Poilâne**? (And how did I become this person?) There are loads of other great country breads on the market. But every now and again, I'll have a Thomas' English muffin. Because I'm real. Just ask J. Lo.

BUTTER: Fresh, sweet, and unsalted. From your local farmers, naturally, or an AOC import, such as **Échiré**. Worth every extra penny.

EGGS: Also try duck eggs every now and then for added variety.

PARMIGIANO OR PECORINO CHEESE: Wrap in a moist tea towel.

CHORIZO (IBÉRICO) AND/OR GUANCIALE: Keep it in the fridge wrapped in parchment. You'll find interesting uses for it everywhere, you'll see.

A FRESH SEASONAL HERB: Wrap in moist paper towels and place in an airtight container. Can last up to two weeks this way.

LEMONS: A few on their vines.

ALCOHOL: And always a bottle of Champagne and/or white wine, and/or beer.

ON DRINKING ALONE

AN INTERVIEW WITH COLUM SHEEHAN

FROM PRIMROSE HILL, LONDON, TO PARK SLOPE, BROOKLYN

S: What are you drinking at the moment?

C: A Maximim Grünhäuser Abstberg Spätlese 2004 from the Von Schubert Wincry.

S: Anything to eat?

C: Tomme Crayeuse and bread. A blissful pairing.

S: Geez. Tell me something, why is it assumed that you've become Charles Bukowski when you crack open a bottle of wine at home, alone?

C: It's a strange ... *(tape recorder breaks down, loud buzzing noises)* ... Protestant approach ... a taboo ... struggle ... *(long beep)* ... closet alcoholic ... flasks of vodka in his underwear drawer ... *(beeeeeeeeeeeeeeeep)* ... beer and baseball is fine ...

(The batteries in my 1993 RadioShack tape recorder have officially exploded. I have now replaced them. He's laughing hysterically.)

S: Sorry about that. So much for my professionalism. Okay, generally speaking of course, perhaps a more salubrious lifestyle is embraced in Europe, and there's far less judgment. They take holidays! Eat fat! Drink wine!

C: There's a more relaxed approach to it all—they've grown up with it and live in wine-producing countries. If the French refer to the magnum as the perfect bottle for two (especially, they add, if your partner isn't drinking a lot), then isn't the 750ml bottle perfect for one?

S: Uh, yes! What do you think of half-bottles?

C: I don't like them. They don't travel well because they're too small and are subject to severe fluctuations in temperature, which is bad for the wine. Their traveling conditions may be less than ideal.

S: Just because a full bottle is open doesn't mean you need to drink the whole bloody thing. What are your thoughts on re-corking and drinking it the next day—or the day after?

C: Great—just shove the cork back in the bottle. Most wine is sturdier than people give it credit for. The reality is that *many* wines actually will taste better the following day, once the wine has breathed through. In fact, many great producers still recommend opening their wine before serving it and letting the bottle rest overnight, with the cork out of the bottle.

S: Where do I store wines if I don't have a wine cellar? In one of those wooden wine racks? Or should I throw it against the wall and use it for kindling? Does a wine bottle always need to be stored on its side at 55 degrees Fahrenheit?

C: How about in a cardboard box and not under the radiator? Those wooden racks are fine. I'm tired of hearing people say that they don't store and age wine because they lack the proper conditions. I have enjoyed more than my share of wines aged on the floor of my closet and they have never been the worse for wear. If you want to age a wine for twenty years, then storage matters, but for a year or two, it won't. The biggest problem that I've had with aging has been with my own patience. Store it in cool place with the least amount of fluctuation in temperature.

S: I enjoy having a rapport with the staff at my local wine shop—but sometimes I need to be quick and don't have time for long-winded didactic lectures on acid balance. It's just me and a pork chop tonight, y'know? As a sommelier, how important, do you think, is getting the pairing right?

C: It's everything. And everything that wine is about. You need that balance of acidity, which is perhaps the most important component when it comes to pairing wine and food. First assess the richness of the dish, then find a wine with the proper level of acidity. Richer foods, more acidity. But all the information of history and geography and ampelography are incidental to what one tastes.

S: If someone spends one hundred dollars on a bottle in a restaurant, that same wine is, what, thirty dollars in a wine shop? And because it'll just be for you, it seems rather economical.

C: It's no secret that a restaurant charges more for their wine than a wine store. For that same money, you can drink a much better wine.

S: When exactly does a decanter become necessary? Because when dining out, sometimes I think it's used just to alert other diners and say, "Hey, look over here, I'm drinking something *really* expensive!"

C: It separates the wine from the sediment for really old wines, which sometimes will be at risk because they'll fall apart.

They're also used for very young wines that you drink before you should, to aerate the wine and open the flavors. An '89 to '90 Barolo is twenty years old, yet still has a lot of developing ahead of it and needs to be decanted. I recently had a '29 Romanée-Conti and it decanted beautifully. It was exuberant. Absolutely stunning.

S: What about wineglasses? People think they're really hip and cool when drinking their wine in tumbler glasses.

C: A Carlo Rossi is great in a tumbler, but a vintage-dated wine needs a nice stem and a large bowl to bring out the nuances. There needs to be the respect of experiencing it when you're drinking it. What's the point?

S: Any particular type of corkscrew?

C: Whatever works.

S: To be honest, no matter what I've learned over the years and no matter how many wine tastings I've been to, courses I've taken, vineyards visited, or hundreds (thousands?) of bottles I've had, I still always feel like a complete ass and know very little. See, after a glass or two, if I don't write all the info down, it's forgotten. Perhaps you can give me one or two phrases that'll keep me in the game so I can continue on as the fake that I am.

C: Ask about the level of *brix* [pronounced "bricks"] at harvest—the measurement of sugar in the grapes prior to harvest. Twenty-three to twenty-four is standard. Respond with subtle surprise to whatever they say.

S: What else?

C: Ask what kind of soil the grapes are grown in. Give a similar response.

S: My friend Camilla Richards has a fantastic boutique hotel in Mougins in the South of France and has an interesting wine list catering to her well-versed and appreciative clientele. She refers to unconventional wine pairings as "the triple bluff." Not the obvious pairing, not the second, but—hey, let's go a step further and break all the rules. And it works. Can you give me one or two of those suggestions?

C: A dessert wine with a savory dish. Richness to richness, acidity to acidity. A goose liver ravioli with a Vin Santo is perfect. An Amarone gets steamrolled by it. But I think I've done a lot of that in your book already.

S: I'm so glad we organized this over the phone. It would be nauseating to read between the lines with all of those LOLs and smiley faces that seem to accompany e-mails these days. LOL. LOL. LOL. What's up with that?

C: I don't do that.

S: I know, thank you. You're my hero.

Colum Sheehan is the general manager and former sommelier of Babbo Ristorante and Enoteca, New York City.

SOURCES

BUON ITALIA
www.buonitalia.com
For bottarga di muggine (dried mullet roe)

CITARELLA
www.citarella.com
For langoustines (seasonal), lobsters, crabmeat

D'ARTAGNAN
www.dartagnan.com
For A5 grade Wagyu (single portions available), foie gras (two slices available but freezes well), caviar, duck fat, small game birds

THE FRESH LOBSTER COMPANY
www.thefreshlobstercompany.com
For sashimi-grade fish, live lobsters, lump crabmeat

GOURMET FOOD STORE
www.gourmetfoodstore.com
For Échiré butter

LA ESPAÑOLA MEATS, INC.

www.laespanolameats.com
For bacalao (salt cod)

URBANI TRUFFLES USA

www.urbanitrufflesusa.com
For truffles, black winter truffle juice

WHOLE FOODS (select stores)

www.wholefoods.com
For bacalao (salt cod)

U.K. SUPPLIERS

In Borough Market

BRINDISA

www.brindisa.co.uk
For bacalao, Ibérico chorizo, Calasperra rice, pimentón de La Vera, membrillo (quince paste)

FURNESS FISH, POULTRY, AND GAME SUPPLIES

www.morecambebayshrimps.com
For all fresh seafood including live lobsters, crabmeat, langoustines; all small game birds

THE GINGER PIG

www.thegingerpig.co.uk
For all meats, guanciale

L. BOOTH, THE WILD MUSHROOM COMPANY

Telephone only: +44(0) 207-376-8666
For all fresh Thai vegetables, including galangal, lemongrass; black winter truffle juice, Amalfi lemons

LE MARCHÉ DU QUARTIER

www.marketquarter.com

For duck fat, fresh foie gras (one slice), truffle juice, seasonal truffles

ORKNEY ROSE

www.orkneyrose.com

For sea urchins (sold individually in season)

REAL FRANCE FINE FOODS

www.realfrance.co.uk

For Échiré butter (available in tiny 50g packages)

SHELL SEEKERS

shellseekers@talk21.com

For most fresh seafood, including hand-dived scallops, live lobsters, calamari, crabmeat

VILLANOVA FOOD

www.villanovafood.com

For bottarga di muggine—available whole and in small (100g) vacu-packs, carta musica (also known as pane carasau)

Other

WWW.CAROLIVA.COM

For worldwide suppliers of 0,4 percent olive oil

HARRODS, HARVEY NICHOLS, SELFRIDGES FOOD HALL

For foie gras portions, truffles, caviar, Wagyu steak (single portions), duck fat, small game birds, quince paste, panko breadcrumbs

MOST ASIAN FOOD MARKETS

For wet tamarind, fresh galangal, palm sugar, dashi, lemongrass, rice paper, crispy duck pancakes, curry leaves

EQUIPMENT

For 5 by 5-inch skillets, small porcelain casserole dishes (molds), and mini
paper cups:

U.S. SUPPLIER
BROADWAY PANHANDLER
www.broadwaypanhandler.com

U.K. SUPPLIER
DIVERTIMENTI
www.divertimenti.co.uk

ACKNOWLEDGMENTS

First and foremost, I'm unsure if this book would have ever come to fruition without my dear friend and mentor, Dan Jones—an extraordinary talent, a genius, really. He's been onboard since this book's inception, when I went to him with a sketchy idea and a horribly written rant. We worked through every story over many, many lunches at Soho House on Greek Street, and with his meticulous guidance, patience, and red pen, he has carried me through to its completion. I have never in my life had such a friend and am deeply and forever grateful.

To an amazing team at HarperCollins: Sarah Burningham, a force and a fantastic woman at the same time. I owe this to her—thanks for taking a chance on me. To Cassie Jones—I am still floored by how fortunate I've been to have worked with the most brilliant editor on my first book (thanks, Sarah!). The whole process was effortlessly yin and yang, eased along by her wicked sense of humor throughout. Her kindness and grace have made this experience pretty much transcendent. I've been very lucky and am deeply grateful. And thank you to the entire team behind the book for their expertise: Johnathan Wilber, Lisa Gallagher, Allison Saltzman, David Sweeney, Lynn Grady, Maggie Sivon, Samantha Hagerbaumer, Paula Szafranski, Lucy Albanese, Joyce Wong, and Nyamekye Waliyaya.

To an extraordinary man, Colum Sheehan, for his staggering wealth of knowledge of wines and for significant contribution.

To the chefs who graciously contributed their time and recipes, no matter how busy they were: Luisa Marelli Valazza, Elena Arzak, Carme Ruscalleda, Ruth Rogers and Rose Gray, and Suzanne Goin.

To Chiara De Santis at Be Translated, for the translations of dozens of e-mails and many complicated recipes from the chefs above. And also to Klancy Miller, Mark Brooke, Miguel A. Gallardo, Baatriz Marim Olaya, Sundari Gabrielle, and Ed Howard, for your time and help with even more e-mail translations.

To Roland Mouret, for lending me the Pigalle dress and Louboutins for the cover shoot; Jimmy Lahoud, for the use of his spectacular home and garden; and to Will Whipple, a great photographer who brought it all together.

My crew of recipe tasters for the endless months of testings in my kitchen at Elsworthy Terrace—but especially to Ed Howard, Lucy Chadwick, Glenn and Lindsay Gregory, Siobhan O'Connor and Olle Kickler, and the fabulous Stableforth family: Abigail, Emily, Alex, and Will.

A very special thanks to Virginia Lehman, Tibi Scheflow, Ruth Provenz, Wendy Gahan, Annie Howarth, Clare Morgan, Mark Giordano, Jeff Googel, and Shauna Mei for their unwavering support over the years and throughout this whole process.

My brother, Joseph, and my sisters, Leonora and Michelle.

And to my mom, the love of my life.

(Oh—and to all the fine folk who have given me so many characters and stories to write about. Thank you so much!)

INDEX

A

Affogato, 176
Aioli, Garlic, 150
Almonds
    Cake, 164
    Marcona, Roasted, Manchego Cheese,
        and Quince Dressing, Frisée
        with, 112
Amaretto, Grilled Peaches with, 90
Anchovies
    Basquian Lemon Shrimp, 113
    Pissaladière, 104–5
    Salsa Verde, 204–5
Apple(s)
    Best Pork Chops and Applesauce, 22–23
    Green, and Yuzu Dipping Sauce,
        Yellowtail Sashimi with, 107
    Turnover, 168–69

B

Bacalao
    Baked Salt Cod Fillet, 199
    Croquettes with Aioli, 100–101
    with Fresh Orange and Black Olives,
        199–200
Bacon
    BLT on Toasted Brioche with Garlic
        Aioli, 150
    Grilled, Lima Bean Salad, and
        Cornbread, Soft-Shell Crabs with,
        87–89

Bagels and Cream Cheese, Home-Cured
    Gravlax with, 144–45
Banana Toffee Mille-Feuille, Warm, 166–67
Basil
    adding to salads, 205
    Pizza Margherita (Not Domino's), 45–47
    Salsa Verde, 204–5
    Vietnamese Summer Rolls, 110–11
Basquian Lemon Shrimp, 113
Bean(s)
    Home-Style Yellow Split Peas, 36
    Lima, Salad, Grilled Bacon, and
        Cornbread, Soft-Shell Crabs with,
        87–89
Bean sprouts
    Jasmin's Pad Thai, 39–41
Beef
    Best Steak au Poivre with Frites, 8–10
    A Big Ol' Burger, 134–36
    Pan-Seared Wagyu Steak, 65
    Pecorino, and Black Olives, Carpaccio of,
        102
    Steak Tartare, 10
Beignets, Warm, 148–49
Berry Jam, Warm, 149
Biscotti, Pignoli, 171
Biscuits, Buttermilk, 50
Bistro classics
    Best Braised Lamb Shank, 12–13
    Best Chicken Pot Pie, 14–15
    Best Crab Cakes, 20–21

Bistro classics (*continued*)
  Best Duck Confit, 17–19
  Best Fish & Chips, 24–25
  Best Mac 'n' Cheese, 11
  Best Pork Chops and Applesauce, 22–23
  Best Steak au Poivre with Frites, 8–10
  Steak Tartare, 10
Bloody Mary, 143
Blueberry
  Pancakes, 141
  Wild, Tart, 174–75
Bottarga, Pasta alla, 124–25
Bread(s)
  Buttermilk Biscuits, 50
  buying, 208
  and Chocolate, 192
  Grilled Sardine Panzanella, 108–9
  Homemade Parker House Rolls,
    120–21
  Naan, Homemade, 37–38
A Brownie, 184–85
Brunch
  Bloody Mary, 143
  BLT on Toasted Brioche with Garlic
    Aioli, 150
  Blueberry Pancakes, 141
  Fried Duck Egg with Guanciale and
    Toast, 146
  Frittata con delle Erbe, 147
  Home-Cured Gravlax with Bagels and
    Cream Cheese, 144–45
  Scrambled Eggs, 142
  Sixties Granola, 151
  Warm Beignets, 148–49
  Warm Berry Jam, 149
Burgers
  A Big Ol', 134–36
  Quarter Pounder with Fries (Not
    McDonald's), 51
Butter, buying, 208
Buttermilk Biscuits, 50
Butterscotch Panna Cotta with
    Roasted Macadamia Nut Praline,
    172–73

C

Cake, 164
Calamar Relleno con Setas y Vegetales
    (Mushroom- and Vegetable-Stuffed
    Squid), 78–79
Carpaccio of Beef, Pecorino, and Black
    Olives, 102
Caviar
  Pasta alla Bottarga, 124–25
  and Smoked Salmon, Croque Monsieur
    with, 68–69
Cazuela de Arroz Langoustines, 130–31
Cheese
  Best Mac 'n,' 11
  Carpaccio of Beef, Pecorino, and Black
    Olives, 102
  Cream, and Bagels, Home-Cured Gravlax
    with, 144–45
  Croque Monsieur with Smoked Salmon
    and Caviar, 68–69
  Manchego, Roasted Marcona Almonds,
    Quince Dressing, Frisée with, 112
  mascarpone, seven uses for, 203–4
  Parmigiano, storing, 209
  Pecorino, storing, 209
  Pizza Margherita (Not Domino's),
    45–47
  Three-, Ravioli with Shaved White
    Truffles, 60–61
  Warm Banana Toffee Mille-Feuille,
    166–67
Chef-inspired recipes
  Calamar Relleno con Setas y Vegetales
    (Mushroom- and Vegetable-Stuffed
    Squid), 78–79
  Clips de Cogollos con Mango (Lettuce
    Heart Clips with Mango), 80–83
  Grilled Peaches with Amaretto, 90
  *Ristretto di Piselli con Gnocchetti di Pane
    all'Uva e Fresco di Capra* (Cream of
    Peas, Raisin Bread Gnocchetti, and
    Fresh Goat Cheese), 84–86
  Soft-Shell Crabs with Lima Bean Salad,
    Grilled Bacon, and Cornbread, 87–89

Chicken
  Fried, with Buttermilk Biscuits
    (Not KFC's), 48–50
  General Tsao's, 30–31
  Jasmin's Pad Thai, 39–41
  Pot Pie, Best, 14–15
Chiles, fresh, drying in oven, 19
Chinese take-out classics
  Cold Sesame Noodles, 32
  Crispy Duck with Warm Fresh Plum
    Sauce, 33–34
  General Tsao's Chicken, 30–31
Chocolate
  Bread and, 192
  A Brownie, 184–85
  buying, 208
  Cookies, Melt-in-Your-Mouth, 186
  Fondant, Warm, 181–82
  Ice Cream Float, 191
  One Big Profiterole, 158–59
  Peanut Butter Cups, 183
  Valrhona, Truffles, 187–90
Clips de Cogollos con Mango (Lettuce Heart
  Clips with Mango), 80–83
Coconut
  Fish Curry, 35
  Rice, 44
Coffee
  Affogato, 176
Confit, Duck, Best, 17–19
Cookies, Melt-in-Your-Mouth Chocolate,
  186
Cornbread, Lima Bean Salad, and Grilled
  Bacon, Soft-Shell Crabs with, 87–89
Crab(s)
  Cakes, Best, 20–21
  Soft-Shell, with Lima Bean Salad,
    Grilled Bacon, and Cornbread,
    87–89
Crème fraîche, seven uses for, 203–4
Crêpes Suzette, 160–61
Croque Monsieur with Smoked Salmon and
  Caviar, 68–69
Croquettes, Bacalao, with Aioli, 100–101

Cupcakes, "There-is-no-way-in-hell-I-am-
  waiting-in-line-for-two-hours," 170
Curry, Coconut Fish, 35

D

Desserts
  Affogato, 176
  Apple Turnover, 168–69
  Bread and Chocolate, 192
  A Brownie, 184–85
  Butterscotch Panna Cotta with Roasted
    Macadamia Nut Praline, 172–73
  Cake, 164
  Chocolate Ice Cream Float, 191
  Crêpes Suzette, 160–61
  Fresh Pineapple Tarte Tatin, 162–63
  Grilled Peaches with Amaretto, 90
  Lemon-Lime Gelato, 165
  Melt-in-Your-Mouth Chocolate Cookies,
    186
  One Big Profiterole, 158–59
  Peanut Butter Cups, 183
  Pignoli Biscotti, 171
  "There-is-no-way-in-hell-I-am-waiting-
    in-line-for-two-hours" Cupcakes, 170
  Valrhona Chocolate Truffles, 187–90
  Warm Banana Toffee Mille-Feuille,
    166–67
  Warm Chocolate Fondant, 181–82
  Wild Blueberry Tart, 174–75
Drinks
  Bloody Mary, 143
  Chocolate Ice Cream Float, 191
  Mojito, 205–6
  The Toby Cecchini, 206
Duck
  Confit, Best, 17–19
  Crispy, with Warm Fresh Plum Sauce,
    33–34
  Egg, Fried, with Guanciale and Toast, 146
  fat, uses for, 200–201
  Foie Gras Stuffing, 198
  Ragu with Pappardelle, 197
  Rillette, 197–98

E

Egg(s), 208
 Duck, Fried, with Guanciale and Toast, 146
 Frittata con delle Erbe, 147
 Scrambled, 142
Escalope of Foie Gras with Wild Mush-
 rooms and Aged Balsamic, 70–71

F

Fast food classics
 Fried Chicken with Buttermilk Biscuits
 (Not KFC's), 48–50
 Pizza Margherita (Not Domino's), 45–47
 Quarter Pounder with Fries (Not
 McDonald's), 51
Fish. *See also* Anchovies
 Bacalao Croquettes with Aioli, 100–101
 Baked Salt Cod Fillet, 199
 & Chips, Best, 24–25
 Croque Monsieur with Smoked Salmon
 and Caviar, 68–69
 Curry, Coconut, 35
 Grilled Sardine Panzanella, 108–9
 Home-Cured Gravlax with Bagels and
 Cream Cheese, 144–45
 Pasta alla Bottarga, 124–25
 Steamed, 201–2
 Wild Seam Bream Seviche, 97
 Yellowtail Sashimi with Green Apple and
 Yuzu Dipping Sauce, 107
Foie Gras
 Clips de Cogollos con Mango (Lettuce
 Heart Clips with Mango), 80–83
 Escalope of, with Wild Mushrooms and
 Aged Balsamic, 70–71
 Stuffing, 198
Fondant, Warm Chocolate, 181–82
Frisée with Manchego Cheese, Roasted
 Marcona Almonds, and Quince
 Dressing, 112
Frittata con delle Erbe, 147
Fritters, Zucchini, with Dill, 106
Fruit. *See also specific fruits*
 Sixties Granola, 151

G

Garlic
 Aioli, 150
 roasted, preparing, 19
Gelato, Lemon-Lime, 165
General Tsao's Chicken, 30–31
Gnocchi, 200
Granola, Sixties, 151
Gravlax, Home-Cured, with Bagels and
 Cream Cheese, 144–45
Grazing
 Bacalao Croquettes with Aioli, 100–101
 Basquian Lemon Shrimp, 113
 Carpaccio of Beef, Pecorino, and Black
 Olives, 102
 Frisée with Manchego Cheese, Roasted
 Marcona Almonds, and Quince
 Dressing, 112
 Grilled Sardine Panzanella, 108–9
 Pissaladière, 104–5
 Sea Scallops with Seaweed Butter,
 98–99
 Vietnamese Summer Rolls, 110–11
 Wild Mushrooms on Grilled Ciabatta
 with Garlic Lemon Aioli, 103
 Wild Seam Bream Seviche, 97
 Yellowtail Sashimi with Green Apple and
 Yuzu Dipping Sauce, 107
 Zucchini Fritters with Dill, 106
Greens
 BLT on Toasted Brioche with Garlic
 Aioli, 150
 Clips de Cogollos con Mango (Lettuce
 Heart Clips with Mango), 80–83
 Eat Your Greens! Three Ways, 132–33
 Frisée with Manchego Cheese, Roasted
 Marcona Almonds, and Quince
 Dressing, 112
 Grilled Lamb Chops with Lemongrass,
 43–44
 Grilled Peaches with Amaretto, 90
 Grilled Sardine Panzanella, 108–9
 Grilled Spatchcocked Spiced Quail,
 128–29

Guanciale
 Pasta con Guanciale e Prezzemolo (Pasta
  with Cured Pig Cheeks and Parsley),
  202
 storing, 209
 and Toast, Fried Duck Egg with, 146

H

Herbs
 adding to salads, 205
 fresh, storing, 209
 Frittata con delle Erbe, 147
 Mojito, 205–6
 Pistou/Pesto, 204
 Salsa Verde, 204–5
 The Toby Cecchini, 206
 Vietnamese Summer Rolls, 110–11
Honey, chestnut, 208

I

Ice Cream
 Affogato, 176
 Float, Chocolate, 191
 One Big Profiterole, 158–59
Indian take-out classics
 Coconut Fish Curry, 35
 Homemade Naan Bread, 37–38
 Home-Style Yellow Split Peas, 36
Ingredients, for pantry and refrigerator,
  207–9

J

Jam, Warm Berry, 149

L

Lamb
 Chops, Grilled, with Lemongrass, 43–44
 Shank, Best Braised, 12–13
Langoustines
 Cazuela de Arroz Langoustines, 130–31
Lemongrass
 Broth, Mussels in, 201
 Grilled Lamb Chops with, 43–44
 Steamed Fish, 201–2

Lemon(s), 209
 -Lime Gelato, 165
 Shrimp, Basquian, 113
Lima Bean Salad, Grilled Bacon, and
  Cornbread, Soft-Shell Crabs with,
  87–89
Lime(s)
 -Lemon Gelato, 165
 Mojito, 205–6
 The Toby Cecchini, 206
Lobster, Roasted, 62–64

M

Macadamia Nut, Roasted, Praline,
  Butterscotch Panna Cotta with,
  172–73
Mac 'n' Cheese, Best, 11
Mango
 Clips de Cogollos con Mango (Lettuce
  Heart Clips with Mango), 80–83
Mascarpone
 seven uses for, 203–4
 Warm Banana Toffee Mille-Feuille,
  166–67
Meat. *See* Beef; Lamb; Pork
Messy meals
 A Big Ol' Burger, 134–36
 Cazuela de Arroz Langoustines, 130–31
 Classic Winter Vegetable Soup, 122–23
 Eat Your Greens! Three Ways, 132–33
 Grilled Spatchcocked Spiced Quail,
  128–29
 Homemade Parker House Rolls, 120–21
 Pasta alla Bottarga, 124–25
 Springtime Soup, 123
 Tagliatelle with Black Truffles, 126–27
Mille-Feuille, Warm Banana Toffee,
  166–67
Mint
 adding to salads, 205
 Mojito, 205–6
 The Toby Cecchini, 206
 Vietnamese Summer Rolls, 110–11
Mojito, 205–6

Mushroom(s)
Aged, and Aged Balsamic, Escalope of
Foie Gras with, 70–71
Best Chicken Pot Pie, 14–15
Calamar Relleno con Setas y Vegetales
(Mushroom- and Vegetable-Stuffed
Squid), 78–79
Wild, on Grilled Ciabatta with Garlic
Lemon Aioli, 103
Mussels
in Lemongrass Broth, 201
Sea Urchin Risotto, 66–67

N

Naan Bread, Homemade, 37–38
Noodles
Cold Sesame, 32
Jasmin's Pad Thai, 39–41
Vietnamese Summer Rolls, 110–11
Nut(s)
A Brownie, 184–85
Cake, 164
Frisée with Manchego Cheese, Roasted
Marcona Almonds, and Quince
Dressing, 112
Macadamia, Roasted, Praline, Butter-
scotch Panna Cotta with, 172–73
Peanut Sauce, 110
Pesto, 204
Pignoli Biscotti, 171
roasting, 19
Sixties Granola, 151

O

Oats
Sixties Granola, 151
Olive oil, buying, 207
Olives
Basquian Lemon Shrimp, 113
Black, and Fresh Orange, Bacalao with,
199–200
Black, Beef, and Pecorino, Carpaccio of, 102
Pissaladière, 104–5
One Big Profiterole, 158–59

Onions
Pissaladière, 104–5
Orange(s)
Crêpes Suzette, 160–61
Fresh, and Black Olives, Bacalao with,
199–200

P

Pad Thai, Jasmin's, 39–41
Pancakes, Blueberry, 141
Panna Cotta, Butterscotch, with Roasted
Macadamia Nut Praline, 172–73
Panzanella, Grilled Sardine, 108–9
Parker House Rolls, Homemade, 120–21
Parsley
adding to salads, 205
Salsa Verde, 204–5
Pasta. *See also* Noodles
alla Bottarga, 124–25
Best Mac 'n' Cheese, 11
Duck Ragu with Pappardelle, 197
Pasta con Guanciale e Prezzemolo (Pasta
with Cured Pig Cheeks and Parsley), 202
Scialatielli con Pomodori Ciliege Arrosti
(Homemade Flat Pasta with Roasted
Cherry Tomatoes), 203
Tagliatelle with Black Truffles, 126–27
Three-Cheese Ravioli with Shaved White
Truffles, 60–61
Pasta con Guanciale e Prezzemolo (Pasta with
Cured Pig Cheeks and Parsley), 202
Peaches, Grilled, with Amaretto, 90
Peanut Butter Cups, 183
Peanut Sauce, 110
Peas
*Ristretto di Piselli con Gnocchetti di Pane
all'Uva e Fresco di Capra* (Cream of
Peas, Raisin Bread Gnocchetti, and
Fresh Goat Cheese), 84–86
Peppercorns, buying, 207
Peppers. *See* Chiles
Pesto/Pistou, 204
Pignoli Biscotti, 171
Pineapple, Fresh, Tarte Tatin, 162–63

Pissaladière, 104–5
Pistou/Pesto, 204
Pizza
  Margherita (Not Domino's), 45–47
  Pissaladière, 104–5
Plum, Fresh, Sauce, Warm, Crispy Duck
  with, 33–34
Pork. *See also* Bacon
  Chops and Applesauce, Best, 22–23
  chorizo, storing, 209
  Fried Duck Egg with Guanciale and
    Toast, 146
  guanciale, storing, 209
  Jasmin's Pad Thai, 39–41
  Pasta con Guanciale e Prezzemolo (Pasta
    with Cured Pig Cheeks and Parsley), 202
Potatoes
  Best Braised Lamb Shank, 12–13
  Best Chicken Pot Pie, 14–15
  Best Fish & Chips, 24–25
  Best Steak au Poivre with Frites, 8–10
  Gnocchi, 200
Pot Pie, Chicken, Best, 14–15
Poultry. *See also* Chicken; Duck
  Foie Gras Stuffing for, 198
  Grilled Spatchcocked Spiced Quail,
    128–29
Praline, Roasted Macadamia Nut,
  Butterscotch Panna Cotta with, 172–73
Profiterole, One Big, 158–59

Q

Quail, Grilled Spatchcocked Spiced, 128–29

R

Ravioli, Three-Cheese, with Shaved White
  Truffles, 60–61
Rice
  Cazuela de Arroz Langoustines, 130–31
  Coconut, 44
  General Tsao's Chicken, 30–31
  Mussels in Lemongrass Broth, 201
  Sea Urchin Risotto, 66–67
Rillette, Duck, 197–98

Risotto, Sea Urchin, 66–67
*Ristretto di Piselli con Gnocchetti di Pane
  all'Uva e Fresco di Capra* (Cream of
  Peas, Raisin Bread Gnocchetti, and
  Fresh Goat Cheese), 84–86
Rolls, Parker House, Homemade, 120–21
Rum
  Cake, 164
  Mojito, 205–6
  The Toby Cecchini, 206

S

Salads
  Frisée with Manchego Cheese, Roasted
    Marcona Almonds, and Quince
    Dressing, 112
  Lima Bean, Grilled Bacon, and Cornbread,
    Soft Shell Crabs with, 87–89
Salmon
  Home-Cured Gravlax with Bagels and
    Cream Cheese, 144–45
  Smoked, and Caviar, Croque Monsieur
    with, 68–69
Salsa Verde, 204–5
Salt, buying, 207
Salt Cod
  Bacalao Croquettes with Aioli, 100–101
  Bacalao with Fresh Orange and Black
    Olives, 199–200
  Fillet, Baked, 199
Sandwiches
  BLT on Toasted Brioche with Garlic
    Aioli, 150
  Croque Monsieur with Smoked Salmon
    and Caviar, 68–69
Sardine, Grilled, Panzanella, 108–9
Sashimi, Yellowtail, with Green Apple and
  Yuzu Dipping Sauce, 107
Sauce, Peanut, 110
Sauce, Tartar, 25
Scallops, Sea, with Seaweed Butter, 98–99
*Scialatielli con Pomodori Ciliege
  Arrosti* (Homemade Flat Pasta with
  Roasted Cherry Tomatoes), 203

Sea bass
   Coconut Fish Curry, 35
   Steamed Fish, 201–2
Seam Bream, Wild, Seviche, 97
Sea Urchin Risotto, 66–67
Seaweed Butter, Sea Scallops with, 98–99
Sesame Noodles, Cold, 32
Seviche, Wild Seam Bream, 97
Shellfish
   Basquian Lemon Shrimp, 113
   Best Crab Cakes, 20–21
   Calamar Relleno con Setas y Vegetales
      (Mushroom- and Vegetable-Stuffed
      Squid), 78–79
   Cazuela de Arroz Langoustines, 130–31
   Jasmin's Pad Thai, 39–41
   Mussels in Lemongrass Broth, 201
   Roasted Lobster, 62–64
   Sea Scallops with Seaweed Butter, 98–99
   Sea Urchin Risotto, 66–67
   Soft-Shell Crabs with Lima Bean Salad,
      Grilled Bacon, and Cornbread, 87–89
   Tom Yum Kung Soup, 42
   Vietnamese Summer Rolls, 110–11
Shrimp
   Basquian Lemon, 113
   Jasmin's Pad Thai, 39–41
   Tom Yum Kung Soup, 42
   Vietnamese Summer Rolls, 110–11
Soups
   *Ristretto di Piselli con Gnocchetti di Pane
      all'Uva e Fresco di Capra* (Cream of
      Peas, Raisin Bread Gnocchetti, and
      Fresh Goat Cheese), 84–86
   Springtime, 123
   Tom Yum Kung, 42
   Winter Vegetable, Classic, 122–23
Split Peas, Yellow, Home-Style, 36
Squash. *See* Zucchini
Squid
   Calamar Relleno con Setas y Vegetales
      (Mushroom- and Vegetable-Stuffed
      Squid), 78–79
   Sea Urchin Risotto, 66–67

Steak
   au Poivre, Best, with Frites, 8–10
   Tartare, 10
   Wagyu, Pan-Seared, 65
Stock, buying, 208
Stuffing, Foie Gras, 198
Summer Rolls, Vietnamese, 110–11

T

Tagliatelle with Black Truffles, 126–27
Take-out classics
   Coconut Fish Curry, 35
   Cold Sesame Noodles, 32
   Crispy Duck with Warm Fresh Plum
      Sauce, 33–34
   Fried Chicken with Buttermilk Biscuits
      (Not KFC's), 48–50
   General Tsao's Chicken, 30–31
   Grilled Lamb Chops with Lemongrass,
      43–44
   Homemade Naan Bread, 37–38
   Home-Style Yellow Split Peas, 36
   Jasmin's Pad Thai, 39–41
   Pizza Margherita (Not Domino's),
      45–47
   Quarter Pounder with Fries (Not
      McDonald's), 51
   Tom Yum Kung Soup, 42
Tart, Wild Blueberry, 174–75
Tartar Sauce, 25
Tarte Tatin, Fresh Pineapple, 162–63
Thai take-out classics
   Grilled Lamb Chops with Lemongrass,
      43–44
   Jasmin's Pad Thai, 39–41
   Tom Yum Kung Soup, 42
"There-is-no-way-in-hell-I-am-waiting-in-
      line-for-two-hours" Cupcakes, 170
The Toby Cecchini, 206
Tomato(es)
   Bloody Mary, 143
   BLT on Toasted Brioche with Garlic
      Aioli, 150
   Duck Ragu with Pappardelle, 197

Pizza Margherita (Not Domino's), 45–47
Scialatielli con Pomodori Ciliege Arrosti
  (Homemade Flat Pasta with Roasted
  Cherry Tomatoes), 203
Vinaigrette, 82
Tom Yum Kung Soup, 42
Truffles
Black, Tagliatelle with, 126–27
White, Shaved, Three-Cheese Ravioli
  with, 60–61
Truffles, Valrhona Chocolate, 187–90
Turnover, Apple, 168–69

V

Vegetable(s). *See also specific vegetables*
Calamar Relleno con Setas y Vegetales
  (Mushroom- and Vegetable-Stuffed
  Squid), 78–79
Springtime Soup, 123
Winter, Soup, Classic, 122–23

Vietnamese Summer Rolls, 110–11
Vinaigrette, Tomato, 82

W

Walnuts
A Brownie, 184–85

Y

Yellow Split Peas, Home-Style, 36
Yellowtail Sashimi with Green Apple and
  Yuzu Dipping Sauce, 107
Yuzu and Green Apple Dipping Sauce,
  Yellowtail Sashimi with, 107

Z

Zucchini
Calamar Relleno con Setas y Vegetales
  (Mushroom- and Vegetable-Stuffed
  Squid), 78–79
Fritters with Dill, 106

ABOUT THE AUTHOR

Suzanne Pirret completed the Grand Diplôme from Le Cordon Bleu, beginning in Paris and ending in London, after having worked in the restaurant industry since she was a very young girl. She is also an actor and a graduate of the American Repertory Theatre Institute at Harvard. An award-winning voice-over artist, she has recorded hundreds of voice-overs and commercials in New York, Los Angeles, and London. This is her first book. She lives in London.